Introduction to Problem Solving

Grades 6–8

Joy Bronston Schackow
Susan O'Connell

The Math Process Standards Series
Susan O'Connell, Series Editor

HEINEMANN
Portsmouth, NH

Heinemann
361 Hanover Street
Portsmouth, NH 03801–3912
www.heinemann.com

Offices and agents throughout the world

The authors and publisher wish to thank those who have generously given permission to reprint borrowed material:

Excerpts from *Principles and Standards for School Mathematics.* Copyright © 2000 by the National Council of Teachers of Mathematics. Reprinted with permission. All rights reserved.

Library of Congress Cataloging-in-Publication Data
Schackow, Joy Bronston.
    Introduction to problem solving : grades 6–8 / Joy Schackow, Susan O'Connell.
        p. cm. — (Math process standards series)
    Includes bibliographical references.
    ISBN-13: 978-0-325-01296-4
    ISBN-10: 0-325-01296-2
    1. Problem solving.   2. Mathematical analysis.   3. Mathematics—Study and teaching (Middle school).   I. O'Connell, Susan.   II. Title.
    QA63.S33 2008
    510.71'2—dc22   2007044324

Editor: Emily Michie Birch
Production coordinator: Elizabeth Valway
Production service: Matrix Productions Inc.
Cover design: Night & Day Design
Cover photography: Joy Bronston Schackow
Composition: Publishers' Design and Production Services, Inc.
CD production: Nicole Russell
Manufacturing: Louise Richardson

Printed in the United States of America on acid-free paper
12   11   10   09   08   ML   1   2   3   4   5

To our families for their love and support
and to the memory of Johnny G.

On the CD-ROM

In order to be effective mathematicians, students need to develop understanding of critical math content. They need to understand number and operations, algebra, measurement, geometry, and data analysis and probability. Through continued study of these content domains, students gain a comprehensive understanding of mathematics as a subject with varied and interconnected concepts. As math teachers, we attempt to provide students with exposure to, exploration in, and reflection about the many skills and concepts that make up the study of mathematics.

Even with a deep understanding of math content, however, students may lack important skills that can assist them in their development as effective mathematicians. Along with content knowledge, students need an understanding of the processes used by mathematicians. They must learn to problem solve, communicate their ideas, reason through math situations, prove their conjectures, make connections between and among math concepts, and represent their mathematical thinking. Development of content alone does not provide students with the means to explore, express, or apply that content. As we strive to develop effective mathematicians, we are challenged to develop both students' content understanding and process skills.

The National Council of Teachers of Mathematics (2000) has outlined critical content and process standards in its *Principles and Standards for School Mathematics* document. These standards have become the roadmap for the development of textbooks, curriculum materials, and student assessments. These standards have provided a framework for thinking about what needs to be taught in math classrooms and how various skills and concepts can be blended together to create a seamless math curriculum. The first five standards outline content standards and expectations related to number and operations, algebra, geometry, measurement, and data analysis and probability. The second five standards outline the process goals of problem solving, reasoning and proof, communication, connections, and representations. A strong understanding of these standards empowers teachers to identify and select activities within their curricula to produce powerful learning. The standards provide a vision for what teachers hope their students will achieve.

This book is a part of a vital series designed to assist teachers in understanding the NCTM Process Standards and the ways in which they impact and guide student learning. An additional goal of this series is to provide practical ideas to support teachers as they ensure that the acquisition of process skills has a critical place in their math instruction. Through this series, teachers will gain an understanding of each process standard as well as gather ideas for bringing that standard to life within their math classrooms. It offers practical ideas for lesson development, implementation, and assessment that work with any curriculum. Each book in the series focuses on a critical process skill in a highlighted grade band and all books are designed to encourage reflection about teaching and learning. The series also highlights the interconnected nature of the process and content standards by showing correlations between them and showcasing activities that address multiple standards.

Students who develop an understanding of content skills and cultivate the process skills that allow them to apply that content understanding become effective mathematicians. Our goal as teachers is to support and guide students as they develop both their content knowledge and their process skills, so they are able to continue to expand and refine their understanding of mathematics. This series is a guide for math educators who aspire to teach students more than math content. It is a guide to assist teachers in understanding and teaching the critical processes through which students learn and make sense of mathematics.

Susan O'Connell
Series Editor

Spending time in classrooms and watching students solve problems is always exciting, and we want to thank the teachers and students who graciously welcomed us into their classrooms. It was a pleasure posing problems, hearing the student discussions, and seeing the excitement generated by the problem-solving experiences. Thanks to the following students who contributed work samples or allowed their photographs to be included in this book: Jessica Aguiniga, Magdalena Camacho, Jordan Dang, Lydia Diaz-Ibarra, Jeniffer Feliciano, Ariel Fetters, David Garcia, Eric Gonzalez, Johnny Gras, Tirea Jones, Eric Landeros, Sara Longoria, Shantell Moses, Yesenia Pena, Andrew Preda, Amber Reiniger, Jerry Seaton, Jessica Toole, Erik Trejo, and Cheryl Wiggins.

And it was a pleasure to collaborate with outstanding teachers as we gathered ideas and insights for this book. Special thanks to these teachers who shared student work samples or allowed us to work side-by-side with them in their classrooms: Nicole Hildebrand from Shields Middle School in Ruskin, FL and Kara Washington from J.B. Martin Middle School in Paradis, LA. A special thanks to Tom Scott, principal of Shields Middle School, Ruskin, Florida, for allowing us to work with Nicole Hildebrand and her wonderful students.

Delving into the NCTM problem-solving process standard has been an exciting project. Special thanks to Emily Birch, our Heinemann editor, for her continued guidance and support throughout the writing of this book, and to Elizabeth Valway, our production editor, and Aaron Downey at Matrix Productions for their valued contributions to the production of both the book and CD.

Most especially, our thanks to our families: Joy's husband Sam and children Mark and Stefanie, and Sue's husband Pat and children Brendan and Katie.

Problem-Solving Standard

Instructional programs from prekindergarten through grade 12 should enable all students to—

■ build new mathematical knowledge through problem solving;

■ solve problems that arise in mathematics and in other contexts;

■ apply and adapt a variety of appropriate strategies to solve problems;

■ monitor and reflect on the process of mathematical problem solving.

Reasoning and Proof Standard

Instructional programs from prekindergarten through grade 12 should enable all students to—

■ recognize reasoning and proof as fundamental aspects of mathematics;

■ make and investigate mathematical conjectures;

■ develop and evaluate mathematical arguments and proofs;

■ select and use various types of reasoning and methods of proof.

---

[1] Standards are listed with the permission of the National Council of Teachers of Mathematics (NCTM). NCTM does not endorse the content or validity of these alignments.

Communication Standard

Instructional programs from prekindergarten through grade 12 should enable all students to—

- organize and consolidate their mathematical thinking through communication;

- communicate their mathematical thinking coherently and clearly to peers, teachers, and others;

- analyze and evaluate the mathematical thinking and strategies of others;

- use the language of mathematics to express mathematical ideas precisely.

Connections Standard

Instructional programs from prekindergarten through grade 12 should enable all students to—

- recognize and use connections among mathematical ideas;

- understand how mathematical ideas interconnect and build on one another to produce a coherent whole;

- recognize and apply mathematics in contexts outside of mathematics.

Representation Standard

Instructional programs from prekindergarten through grade 12 should enable all students to—

- create and use representations to organize, record, and communicate mathematical ideas;

- select, apply, and translate among mathematical representations to solve problems;

- use representations to model and interpret physical, social, and mathematical phenomena.

NCTM Content Standards and Expectations for Grades 6–8

NUMBER AND OPERATIONS

	Expectations
Instructional programs from prekindergarten through grade 12 should enable all students to—	**In grades 6–8 all students should—**
Understand numbers, ways of representing numbers, relationships among numbers, and number systems	• work flexibly with fractions, decimals, and percents to solve problems; • compare and order fractions, decimals, and percents efficiently and find their approximate locations on a number line; • develop meaning for percents greater than 100 and less than 1; • understand and use ratios and proportions to represent quantitative relationships; • develop an understanding of large numbers and recognize and appropriately use exponential, scientific, and calculator notation; • use factors, multiples, prime factorization, and relatively prime numbers to solve problems; • develop meaning for integers and represent and compare quantities with them.
Understand meanings of operations and how they relate to one another	• understand the meaning and effects of arithmetic operations with fractions, decimals, and integers; • use the associative and commutative properties of addition and multiplication and the distributive property of multiplication over addition to simplify computations with integers, fractions, and decimals; • understand and use the inverse relationships of addition and subtraction, multiplication and division, and squaring and finding square roots to simplify computations and solve problems.

	Expectations
Instructional programs from prekindergarten through grade 12 should enable all students to—	**In grades 6–8 all students should—**
Compute fluently and make reasonable estimates	• select appropriate methods and tools for computing with fractions and decimals from among mental computation, estimation, calculators or computers, and paper and pencil, depending on the situation, and apply the selected methods;
	• develop and analyze algorithms for computing with fractions, decimals, and integers and develop fluency in their use;
	• develop and use strategies to estimate the results of rational-number computations and judge the reasonableness of the results;
	• develop, analyze, and explain methods for solving problems involving proportions, such as scaling and finding equivalent ratios.

ALGEBRA

	Expectations
Instructional programs from prekindergarten through grade 12 should enable all students to—	**In grades 6–8 all students should—**
Understand patterns, relations, and functions	• represent, analyze, and generalize a variety of patterns with tables, graphs, words, and, when possible, symbolic rules;
	• relate and compare different forms of representation for a relationship;
	• identify functions as linear or nonlinear and contrast their properties from tables, graphs, or equations.
Represent and analyze mathematical situations and structures using algebraic symbols	• develop an initial conceptual understanding of different uses of variables;

	Expectations
Instructional programs from prekindergarten through grade 12 should enable all students to—	**In grades 6–8 all students should—**
	• explore relationships between symbolic expressions and graphs of lines, paying particular attention to the meaning of intercept and slope;
	• use symbolic algebra to represent situations and to solve problems, especially those that involve linear relationships;
	• recognize and generate equivalent forms for simple algebraic expressions and solve linear equations.
Use mathematical models to represent and understand quantitative relationships	• model and solve contextualized problems using various representations, such as graphs, tables, and equations.
Analyze change in various contexts	• use graphs to analyze the nature of changes in quantities in linear relationships.

GEOMETRY

	Expectations
Instructional programs from prekindergarten through grade 12 should enable all students to—	**In grades 6–8 all students should—**
Analyze characteristics and properties of two- and three-dimensional geometric shapes and develop mathematical arguments about geometric relationships	• precisely describe, classify, and understand relationships among types of two- and three-dimensional objects using their defining properties;
	• understand relationships among the angles, side lengths, perimeters, areas, and volumes of similar objects;
	• create and critique inductive and deductive arguments concerning geometric ideas and relationships, such as congruence, similarity, and the Pythagorean relationship.

	Expectations
Instructional programs from prekindergarten through grade 12 should enable all students to—	**In grades 6–8 all students should—**
Specify locations and describe spatial relationships using coordinate geometry and other representational systems	• use coordinate geometry to represent and examine the properties of geometric shapes; • use coordinate geometry to examine special geometric shapes, such as regular polygons or those with pairs of parallel or perpendicular sides.
Apply transformations and use symmetry to analyze mathematical situations	• describe sizes, positions, and orientations of shapes under informal transformations such as flips, turns, slides, and scaling; • examine the congruence, similarity, and line or rotational symmetry of objects using transformations.
Use visualization, spatial reasoning, and geometric modeling to solve problems	• draw geometric objects with specified properties, such as side lengths or angle measures; • use two-dimensional representations of three-dimensional objects to visualize and solve problems such as those involving surface area and volume; • use visual tools such as networks to represent and solve problems; • use geometric models to represent and explain numerical and algebraic relationships; • recognize and apply geometric ideas and relationships in areas outside the mathematics classroom, such as art, science, and everyday life.

	Expectations
Instructional programs from prekindergarten through grade 12 should enable all students to—	**In grades 6–8 all students should—**
Understand measurable attributes of objects and the units, systems, and processes of measurement	• understand both metric and customary systems of measurement; • understand relationships among units and convert from one unit to another within the same system; • understand, select, and use units of appropriate size and type to measure angles, perimeter, area, surface area, and volume.
Apply appropriate techniques, tools, and formulas to determine measurements	• use common benchmarks to select appropriate methods for estimating measurements; • select and apply techniques and tools to accurately find length, area, volume, and angle measures to appropriate levels of precision; • develop and use formulas to determine the circumference of circles and the area of triangles, parallelograms, trapezoids, and circles and develop strategies to find the area of more-complex shapes; • develop strategies to determine the surface area and volume of selected prisms, pyramids, and cylinders; • solve problems involving scale factors, using ratio and proportion; • solve simple problems involving rates and derived measurements for such attributes as velocity and density.

NCTM Process
Standards and
Expectations

	Expectations
Instructional programs from prekindergarten through grade 12 should enable all students to—	**In grades 6–8 all students should—**
Formulate questions that can be addressed with data and collect, organize, and display relevant data to answer them	• formulate questions, design studies, and collect data about a characteristic shared by two populations or different characteristics within one population; • select, create, and use appropriate graphical representations of data, including histograms, box plots, and scatterplots.
Select and use appropriate statistical methods to analyze data	• find, use, and interpret measures of center and spread, including mean and interquartile range; • discuss and understand the correspondence between data sets and their graphical representations, especially histograms, stem-and-leaf plots, box plots, and scatterplots.
Develop and evaluate inferences and predictions that are based on data	• use observations about differences between two or more samples to make conjectures about the populations from which the samples were taken; • make conjectures about possible relationships between two characteristics of a sample on the basis of scatterplots of the data and approximate lines of fit; • use conjectures to formulate new questions and plan new studies to answer them.
Understand and apply basic concepts of probability	• understand and use appropriate terminology to describe complementary and mutually exclusive events; • use proportionality and a basic understanding of probability to make and test conjectures about the results of experiments and simulations; • compute probabilities for simple compound events, using such methods as organized lists, tree diagrams, and area models.

The Problem-Solving Standard

Solving problems is not only a goal of learning mathematics but also a major means of doing so.

—National Council of Teachers of Mathematics,
Principles and Standards for School Mathematics

Why Focus on Problem Solving?

Traditionally, problem solving was viewed as a distinct topic, introduced to students after they had mastered basic skills. In today's classrooms, however, problem solving is recognized as the central focus of mathematics instruction. The ability to solve problems is the ultimate goal of mathematics. It is why we teach students to add, subtract, multiply, and divide. It is why we teach them to work with fractions, decimals, measurement, and geometry. Our goal is not for students to perform isolated computations, but rather to be able to apply their varied math skills to solve problems. But problem solving is more than just a goal of learning mathematics; it is also a critical process, woven across the entire mathematics curriculum, through which students are able to explore and understand mathematics (NCTM 2000, 52). Through problem-solving experiences, students learn to challenge their thinking about data and probability, test their ideas about numbers and operations, apply their skills in geometry and measurement, and evaluate their understandings of algebra. Through problem-solving tasks, students develop an understanding of math content and ultimately use that content understanding to find solutions to problems. Problem solving is both the process by which students explore mathematics and the goal of learning mathematics.

One objective of problem-solving instruction is to enable students to use their repertoire of math skills to solve problems. But it takes more than isolated math skills

1

to be an effective problem solver. It also takes a variety of thinking skills that allow students to organize ideas, select appropriate strategies, and determine the reasonableness of solutions. It takes an understanding of how to use and adapt strategies to fit the problem situation. And it takes an ability to reflect on how we solve problems to help us better understand our own thought processes and identify why we select and apply various strategies.

In the past, problem solving may have been viewed as an isolated assignment (e.g., a list of word problems), but today problem solving has an integrated role in the math classroom. Teachers begin lessons by posing a problem, then skills and strategies are developed throughout the lesson as the problem is explored, and those newly acquired skills allow students to successfully find a solution. Problem solving becomes both the starting point and the ending point to well-balanced mathematics lessons. Developing students' computational skills is important, but teaching those skills in a problem-solving context ensures that students not only understand the skill but see the meaningfulness of learning the skill and understand how to apply it to real-world situations. "Problem solving is the process by which students experience the power and usefulness of mathematics in the world around them" (NCTM 1989, 75).

What Is the Problem-Solving Process Standard?

The National Council of Teachers of Mathematics (NCTM) has developed standards to support and guide teachers as they develop classroom lessons and create activities to build their students' mathematical understandings. Some of those standards delineate the content to be addressed in the math classroom, while other standards address the processes by which students explore and use mathematics. Problem solving is a critical math process, and the components of the NCTM Problem Solving Process Standard reflect its complex nature. Instructional programs (NCTM 2000, 52) should enable students to:

- build new mathematical knowledge through problem solving;

- solve problems that arise in mathematics and in other contexts;

- apply and adapt a variety of appropriate strategies to solve problems;

- monitor and reflect on the process of mathematical problem solving.

Throughout this book, we explore ways to assist students in building new math knowledge through problem-solving tasks. Highlighted problem-solving activities may be presented in math contexts as well as real-world contexts. We explore, in depth, the various problem-solving strategies that support students in finding solutions, and we identify techniques for helping students reflect on and monitor their problem solving. We will dive into the NCTM process standard of problem solving in order to better understand it and find ways to bring it to life within our classrooms.

Creating Effective Problem Solvers

In our early experiences with teaching problem solving, we began much like our own teachers had, assigning problems to students and expecting them to be able to solve the problems on their own. We quickly recognized our students' anxiety and frustration. We soon learned that assigning problems and then correcting those problems did not create successful problem solvers. We began to break down the skills needed to solve problems and find opportunities to guide students in developing some specific strategies to help them organize their thinking. Through a combination of modeling, providing opportunities for exploration, facilitating discussions about thinking, and prompting students to reflect on their experiences, we observed the growing efficiency with which our students solved problems. The more they explored and analyzed problem-solving strategies, the more successful they became. Surprisingly, not just the most capable of our students showed progress, but all of them did. As we demonstrated various strategies to attack problems and began to let our students see math problems through visual and hands-on demonstrations, their skills improved. And our skills improved, too! The more comfortable we became at teaching problem solving, the more confident we became about our abilities to help our students understand a process that had once seemed so complicated and abstract.

With an understanding of the problem-solving process and a repertoire of strategies to assist our students in dealing with problem situations, our anxiety and frustration lessens and our enthusiasm and confidence grow. Not all students can become effective problem solvers on their own, but with the help of a confident and capable teacher, all students can significantly improve their problem-solving abilities.

Developing Skills and Attitudes

Developing students' problem-solving abilities is a challenging and complex task. It requires attention to the building of mathematical skills and thinking processes as well as attention to the development of positive attitudes toward problem solving. Both skills and attitudes must be strengthened to produce truly effective problem solvers.

Problem solving is a process that requires students to follow a series of steps to find a solution. Although some students may intuitively follow a process, many students need to be taught how to proceed to reach a solution. Another important goal in teaching students to solve problems is assisting them in developing strategies or plans for solving problems. Although choosing a mathematical operation—addition, subtraction, multiplication, or division—is frequently the way to solve a problem, alternate strategies are often needed. Helping students learn strategies such as drawing pictures, finding patterns, making tables, making lists, guessing and checking, working backward, or using logical reasoning gives students a wide variety of strategies to employ during problem solving. Problem solving requires this knowledge of strategies as well as the ability to determine when each strategy would be best used. The more our students practice these strategies, the more confident they become in their ability to solve problems and apply mathematics in meaningful ways.

The development of a positive attitude toward problem solving is crucial to student success. As teachers, we are instrumental in helping our students develop the attitudes needed to become successful problem solvers.

Problem Solving Requires Patience. It is not always possible to find a quick answer, and quick answers are often incorrect. Problem solving is not judged on speed but on the reasonableness of the final solution.

Problem Solving Requires Persistence. Students may need to try several strategies before finding one that will work. Students must have confidence that they can find a solution, even if the pathway is not immediately apparent.

Problem Solving Requires Risk Taking. Students need to be willing to try their "hunches," hoping that they may lead to a solution. Students must feel comfortable making mistakes, as problem solving is a process filled with mistakes that often lead to solutions.

Problem Solving Requires Cooperation. Students must often be willing to share ideas, build on one another's thoughts, and work together to find a solution.

Students become successful problem solvers when they are instructed in a climate that rewards patience, persistence, risk taking, and cooperation. As teachers, we have a critical role in establishing a positive climate for problem-solving instruction.

How This Book Will Help You

This book is designed to help you better understand the NCTM problem-solving standard. It explores problem solving as both a process through which students learn mathematics and a skill that enables them to apply the mathematics they have learned. The mathematical goals of students in grades 6 through 8 are specifically addressed, and practical ideas for helping students become effective problem solvers are shared.

This book presents ideas for developing a problem-centered approach to teaching mathematics within your classroom. We will see how problem solving can set a context for learning math skills, can excite and engage students, and can help students discover insights and better understand math ideas. We explore ways in which problem solving enriches our math classrooms and nurtures enthusiasm, curiosity, and insight.

Within this book you will find a variety of ideas to help you better understand the problem-solving process, as well as specific strategies including Choose an Operation; Find a Pattern; Make a Table; Make an Organized List; Draw a Picture or Diagram; Guess, Check, and Revise; Use Logical Reasoning; and Work Backward. These strategies help students organize their thinking, figure out ways to approach and simplify problems, and ultimately find their way to solutions. We explore practical ways to support our students as they develop these thinking skills, knowing that the groundwork for each strategy is laid in the elementary grades but that students in grades 6 through 8 refine their use of these strategies and engage in tasks requiring a more sophisticated understanding. As we investigate a variety of problem-solving strategies, we delve into their underlying skills in order to unearth the complexity and importance of each strategy. A variety of activities that are appropriate for students in the middle grades are shared for each strategy. Specific grade levels are not indicated on each activity, as problem-solving skills do not develop by grade level, but rather depend on students' prior knowledge and previous exposure to each strategy. Teacher tips are shared, highlighting important points to emphasize when working with students. Many examples of student work are presented, including samples of students' communication about their problem solving. The work samples illustrate the progression of problem-solving skills, and the writing samples offer a glimpse into students' thinking as their skills develop.

Once we have explored the problem-solving standard in depth, you will see how it connects to the math content standards in the chapter *Problem Solving Across the Content Standards*. Through sample classroom activities, we explore the interconnectedness of the content and process standards. We discuss sample problem-solving tasks that blend with math content for grades 6 through 8 in numbers and operations, algebra, geometry, measurement, and data and probability. Student work is shared to illustrate these lessons, and you will be asked to reflect on the combined teaching of math content and the problem-solving process. In Chapter 11 we discuss ways to assess problem solving, including the use of rubrics to assess students' skills.

While this book is designed to help you better understand the NCTM Problem Solving Standard and to provide you with practical ideas and classroom activities related to the standard, it is also intended to stimulate thought about teaching and learning. Following each chapter, several questions prompt you to reflect on the content of the chapter whether alone or with a group of your colleagues. If you take a moment to reflect on the ideas presented and relate them to your teaching experiences and your observations of your students, you will find it easier to process the ideas and apply them to your students' specific needs.

A very important component of this book is its inclusion of the practical resources needed to implement the ideas explored throughout the chapters. The accompanying CD is filled with a variety of teacher-ready materials to help you implement a problem-solving program in your school or classroom. Checklists, evaluation forms, scoring keys, and icons are all available, as well as a variety of practice problems for your students. The practice problems range from simple to complex. Select those activities that suit your students' level of expertise, and continue to challenge your students with more sophisticated thinking as their skills improve. And the activities and resources on the CD can be easily modified to suit your students' specific needs. Before printing the activity pages, simply change the data to make it less or more challenging, or insert familiar names and places to engage and motivate your students. The editable feature of the CD allows you to easily create a library of problems that are perfect for your students.

This book was developed as a result of our readings about problem-solving theory, our reflections on current practices, and our observations on the progress of students in varied classroom settings. As a result of both research and practice, we have adapted and modified some common problem-solving techniques, developed some new activities to support problem-solving instruction, and highlighted resources and activities that are particularly effective for students in grades 6 through 8. It is hoped that this book will enhance your understanding of the problem-solving standard and provide you with insights and practical ideas to develop your students' problem-solving skills. When we, as teachers, better understand the complexity and importance of problem solving, we are better able to identify, select, and design meaningful tasks for our students. It is hoped that the varied instructional practices highlighted in this book will assist you in developing your students' skills and expanding your own understandings. Most certainly, as we reflect on and develop our teaching skills, our students' problem-solving skills will increase as well.

Questions for Discussion

1. When you were a student in the middle grades, were you taught how to solve math problems or just assigned problems to solve? How did you feel about math problem solving as a student in the math classroom? In what ways do your past experiences and attitudes about problem solving affect your teaching of problem solving?

2. If students show competence with computational skills but lack problem-solving skills, how might it affect their math achievement? What possible problems might they experience?

3. What attitudes are essential for effective problem solving? How might you support students in developing these attitudes?

4. What skills are essential for effective problem solving? How might you help your students acquire those skills?

CHAPTER 1

Building Math Understanding Through Problem Solving

A problem-centered approach to teaching mathematics uses interesting and well-selected problems to launch mathematical lessons and engage students. In this way, new ideas, techniques, and mathematical relationships emerge and become the focus of discussion.

—National Council of Teachers of Mathematics,
Principles and Standards for School Mathematics

"Math was boring!" is a comment heard from many adults remembering endless worksheets and rote textbook assignments. For many of us, math was a process of memorizing facts and procedures and plugging numbers into formulas. There was nothing memorable or exciting about activities in our math classrooms. We completed tasks without even thinking about the meaning of what we were doing. We were bored by the process, hazy in our understanding of the concepts, and unsure of how to apply the skills to problem situations. We want our students to have a different math experience. We want them to be actively engaged in our lessons, excited to explore math ideas, and challenged to reason and problem solve about mathematics. We need more than worksheets to accomplish that!

In today's classrooms, our goal is to help our students use their math knowledge to solve problems rather than to mechanically perform computations. Problem solving is both a goal and a vehicle for our students. Our goal is for them to apply their understanding of math concepts and skills to find solutions to the varied problems they might face, and the problem-solving experiences are the vehicle through which our students are able to explore, discuss, and develop a variety of math skills. We want our students to learn *about* problem solving as well as learn *through* problem solving. We want more for our students than simply having them memorize a series of math skills and concepts. Recent research and professional discussions support the power of problem-centered instruction (Hiebert et al., 1997; Lester and Charles, 2003; Van de Walle and Lovin, 2005). We have recognized its value in helping students better understand important math ideas. Problem-centered instruction is a significant tool for helping students examine, predict, observe, discover, and ultimately use mathematics.

Teaching Math Through Problems

Lecture, combined with drill and practice, have been the typical teaching scenario in math classrooms. Our teachers identified key ideas and told us what we needed to know, and then they asked us to practice the skills until we had committed them to memory. Students with strong rote skills were able to effectively memorize facts and ideas, often realizing later that they did not understand the processes they had memorized. Students with poor rote skills struggled with memorizing ideas that had no meaning to them and often became frustrated and disenchanted with mathematics. In recent years we have recognized that problem-solving tasks motivate and engage students in a way that lecture and drill-and-practice tasks are unable to do. Students are naturally inquisitive. They like to explore, investigate, and hypothesize. They become excited and energized by new problems. And problem-solving tasks provide our students with opportunities to explore and understand the formulas and algorithms that we were asked to simply memorize. Rather than classrooms in which students are bored with rote facts and formulas, we are striving for classrooms in which our students are excited about math, discover math ideas, and continually build on their math knowledge. Through problem-solving tasks, we are able to transform our classrooms from lecture halls to laboratories.

In problem-centered instruction, rather than telling students key math ideas, the teacher poses problems to engage students in exploration and promote thinking about the important mathematical concepts. Students explore problems with partners or groups and are guided in that exploration by the teacher. Students are actively engaged in learning. They are asked to communicate their ideas, share their insights, apply their previously learned knowledge to new situations, reflect on their experiences, and ultimately discover new math ideas. Through problem tasks, new knowledge is built on existing knowledge. In problem-based instruction, the process of learning is as important as the content being learned. Students are learning new ideas but are also learning "how" to learn new ideas.

A Look at Problem-Centered Instruction

In problem-centered instruction, problems become a starting point for student learning. The problem investigation sets the context through which students are challenged to use their already acquired skills to develop new understandings. As students look at a concept or skill in a problem context, they often formulate questions, test ideas, and ultimately grow to better understand the concept. When exploring the concept of area, for example, students might be challenged to find the area of a triangle. Rather than being told the formula, they work together to use their understandings about finding the area of a square, their spatial sense, and their knowledge of operations to figure out a way to find the unknown area. As they dive into the task, they begin to better understand the concept of area. Sixth graders shared their strategies for finding the area of a trapezoid with these insights:

"You could separate it into two triangles and find the area of each. Then you would add them together."
"Both triangles would have the same height. Only the bases would be different."
"Since only the bases are different, we would have $\frac{1}{2}b_1h + \frac{1}{2}b_2h$. So we could multiply $\frac{1}{2}h(b_1 + b_2)$."
"It's like finding the average of the bases times the height."

Through their own investigations, discussions, and insights, these students were able to process the concept of area and determine a way to calculate the area of a trapezoid. Now, perhaps even before it appears in their textbooks, they have begun to discover the formula for finding the area of a trapezoid and it makes sense to them! Through active involvement in exploring problem situations, students are challenged to begin with what they know about math and through the exploration, build on that understanding to create new and more refined understandings.

Problem-solving tasks require the application of math skills. During problem-solving tasks, students are challenged to move beyond simply solving algorithms. Students are challenged to determine how to solve a problem, and they see real examples of the usefulness of math skills. Rather than adding fractions on worksheets, students see the application of adding fractions as they figure out how many pizzas they will need if John and Steven each eat $\frac{1}{5}$ pizza, Alex eats $\frac{1}{3}$ pizza, and Jamie eats $\frac{1}{4}$ pizza. Would one pizza be enough? The fractions become more than just numbers—they now represent a real problem, and the skill of adding fractions becomes relevant.

Selecting Meaningful Tasks

Problem-based instruction, however, is more than simply posing a problem and asking students to solve it. In problem-centered instruction, teachers are challenged to select appropriate tasks, guide students as they engage in the tasks, and assess their understanding of the mathematics. These essential teacher responsibilities influence the success of the problem-solving activity.

Selecting tasks that lead students to important math learning is fundamental. We may want students to discover a formula, learn to organize information for analysis, or apply computational skills or conceptual understanding to real or mathematical situations. Good problems set the stage for our students to explore and discover significant math ideas. If selected carefully, problem-solving tasks can motivate and engage students in learning math, can illustrate the application of math skills, can support students in the development of new math understanding, and can provide assessment of students' strengths and weaknesses. Meaningful tasks do not need to be lengthy and can be set in a math context or a real-world context, but they need to address important math skills and promote thought about those skills. A look at content standards and indicators will provide you with ideas of critical skills.

Problem-solving tasks can set a context for the learning of a skill or can challenge students to apply already learned skills. Teachers might reinforce place value concepts by asking students to list all of the different ways they could have $3285.16 using bills and coins. Exploring this scenario will reinforce base-ten concepts, if students are allowed to use only one-, ten-, hundred-, and thousand-dollar bills, as well as dimes and pennies. As students explore and discuss options with teammates, they will find that they could have 3,285 one-dollar bills and 16 pennies, but they could also have 32 hundred-dollar bills, 84 one-dollar bills, and 116 pennies. Students will likely be surprised at just how many possibilities exist, and they can challenge each other to see who can find the most.

Since mathematics is about both content and process, problem-solving activities can lead students to insights about either. Content insights might include discoveries about the relationship between area and perimeter as students explore the number of students who can sit around ten tables. While the area (10 square units) does not change, the configuration of the tables changes the perimeters. In addition, problem tasks support students' development of process skills such as ways to represent information, organize information, observe data, and draw conclusions. As students work to find all of the possible combinations when they roll three number cubes (dice) in a probability exploration, they use ways to organize the data to be sure they have not missed any combinations and find ways to record the data so they can draw conclusions about their findings. Through the selection of appropriate problems, students can be challenged to develop and refine their thinking about math content and processes.

The Role of Communication

Guiding students as they explore problems is critical to the success of problem-centered instruction. Support comes in many shapes and sizes. As we observe students during problem tasks, we look for cues to let us know when support or encouragement is needed as frustration sets in or when additional challenges are appropriate. Through questioning to guide their thinking or stimulate ideas or through class debriefing to highlight discoveries, teachers play an active role in ensuring that students are thinking as they work and are learning from the experience.

When we observe students solving problems, we often notice students who are intuitively able to apply strategies as they work through a problem. Others, however, appear to be perplexed as to how to tackle the problem, unable to organize the data in a way that will help them understand it. A goal during problem-solving tasks is to glean insights from those who are using appropriate strategies, help some students identify what they are intuitively doing, and help others gain insight into reasonable approaches for problem-solving tasks. Language in the math classroom is a key for helping students recognize their own and each other's thinking. It makes thinking visible within the classroom.

Through teacher talk, we introduce the task, clarify the question, and guide students in the investigation. After posing the problem, we might clarify it using some examples to help students understand their task. As students work together to solve problems, we ask questions to stimulate thought or redirect efforts. Our words are influential in helping students discover ideas.

Student talk is also a critical component of problem-based instruction. Students should work with partners or groups to foster math talk about their thinking. Through partner and group work we allow students to struggle with ideas and build on each other's insights or allow a natural form of tutoring to occur as some students explain their insights to others. By facilitating class discussions we allow students to express their thoughts and insights and allow others to hear their ideas and meld them into their own. By asking students to share their solutions and approaches, we allow opportunities for all students to see multiple solutions and approaches as well as to hear related ideas as they work to support their own findings.

In problem-centered instruction, the goal is not just a correct answer, although we do love correct answers! The goal is to explore a task, determine a strategy to get to a solution, and learn about math along the way. Students might find varied, but equally reasonable, ways to get to a solution. Allowing students to report about their insights and share their strategies is important in extending the understanding of all students within the classroom. Even wrong answers or illogical strategies are part of the learning process in problem-based instruction. Errors often lead to insights for students and certainly help us better understand our students' thinking.

Figure 1–1 *Working with a partner fosters math talk about students' thinking.*

A Look at a Problem-Based Lesson

Students discover many key math ideas when given opportunities to problem solve and discuss their observations. Miss Stallard gave the following problem to her sixth-grade class:

> **Mr. Perez bought 4 dozen cookies for his Spanish class' Cinco de Mayo celebration. The students only ate $\frac{1}{3}$ of the cookies, so Mr. Perez put the remaining cookies in the teachers' lounge. When he returned after school, $\frac{3}{4}$ of the cookies he had left in the teachers' lounge were gone. What part of the cookies Mr. Perez bought was left uneaten after school? Explain how you solved the problem.**

Miss Stallard began by posing the problem to the class. In order to clarify the task, she asked students to work in pairs or small groups to think about how they might get started with solving this problem. After a few minutes, she asked the students to share their thoughts. Lisa began by suggesting changing 4 dozen cookies to 48 cookies. Michael said that he didn't think they had to do that. "Why can't we just leave it as 4 dozen?" Miss Stallard suggested that Michael try solving the problem using 4 dozen, and Lisa use 48 cookies. "We can compare and see if the problem can be worked both ways." As students made suggestions for needed steps, Miss Stallard recorded them on the board:

- Find out how many cookies the Spanish class ate.

- Figure out how many cookies Mr. Perez put in the teachers' lounge.

- See how many cookies were left at the end of the day.

Miss Stallard then asked students to solve the problem with their partners and to record their work, solutions, and explanations of how they solved the problem. Students had access to paper, pencils, calculators, and various manipulatives. Miss Stallard moved through the room to monitor and support students as they worked on the problem. Lisa and her partner began by dividing 48 by 3. When Miss Stallard asked them why they had done that, they explained that they were finding how many cookies the Spanish class ate. Many of the groups began in a similar manner. However, a few pairs seemed uncertain about how to begin. Miss Stallard suggested that they draw a picture of the cookies or model them with manipulatives. Some immediately began drawing small circles to represent cookies. One group decided to use two-color counters. They carefully counted out 48 counters and arranged them in 3 rows of 16. They told Miss Stallard that they were making uneaten 'cookies' yellow and eaten 'cookies' red. Miss Stallard asked the students to show her what happened in Spanish class. They made one row of 'cookies' (16) red and said that those were the ones eaten in class. Miss Stallard asked them how they knew that. Eric replied, "It's $\frac{1}{3}$ of the cookies, so 1 out of 3 rows."

After allowing the students to work with their partners, discuss their ideas, and determine the fraction of cookies that still remained, Miss Stallard asked each pair to compare their answers with the pair sitting across from them and to explain to each other how they came up with their solutions. Miss Stallard moved through the classroom to listen and observe as pairs shared and explained their solutions. Miss Stallard then brought the whole class together for a discussion of their insights.

Shelley and Carly began by explaining that they had found $\frac{1}{3} \times 48$ cookies and then subtracted the 16 cookies from the original 48 to find that 32 cookies were left after Spanish class. Miss Stallard asked if anyone had found the 32 cookies another way. Jonathan said, "We knew that if the class ate $\frac{1}{3}$ of the cookies, then there were $\frac{2}{3}$ left, and $\frac{2}{3}$ of 48 = 32 cookies left." Miss Stallard asked Jonathan how he knew that $\frac{2}{3}$ of the cookies were left. He replied, "All the cookies are $\frac{3}{3}$, so if they ate $\frac{1}{3}$, $\frac{3}{3} - \frac{1}{3} = \frac{2}{3}$."

Next, Miss Stallard asked students to share what they did once they knew that there were 32 cookies left after Spanish class. Victoria volunteered to come to the board and showed how she had multiplied $\frac{3}{4} \times 32 = 24$, so 24 cookies were in the teachers' lounge. Her conclusion was that there were $\frac{24}{48}$ or $\frac{1}{2}$ of the cookies left. Paul raised his hand and said, "That's not right. The teachers *ate* 24 cookies, so there were only 8 left. So $\frac{8}{48}$ or $\frac{1}{6}$ of the cookies were left." Miss Stallard asked if anyone had found out that there were 8 cookies left using a different way. Jessica raised her hand and said, "It's like Jonathan said before. If the teachers ate $\frac{3}{4}$ of the 32 cookies, then there was $\frac{1}{4}$ left, and $32 \div 4 = 8$." Garrett asked, "Why did you divide by 4?" Jessica replied, "That's the same as multiplying by $\frac{1}{4}$, so $\frac{1}{4} \times 32 = 8$."

Miss Stallard asked Mindy and Keisha to share how they had used the two-color counters. The girls decided to draw a picture on the board to show what they had done. They began by drawing 3 rows of 16 counters to represent the original 48 cookies; one row was red to show that they had been eaten and the other 2 rows were yellow. Then they separated the 32 yellow counters into 4 groups of 8. Keisha explained, "We separated them into 4 equal groups because we wanted to see how much was left after $\frac{3}{4}$ were eaten. One group of 8 was left, so there were $\frac{8}{48}$ or $\frac{1}{6}$ of the original cookies left." As she explained, Keisha showed how all of the 48 counters could be put into 6 equal groups of 8, and how all but the 8 'cookies' left after school were red. Only $\frac{1}{6}$ remained yellow.

Although most of the students had changed the original 4 dozen cookies to 48, Michael and Jeremy kept the cookies in dozens. Miss Stallard asked them to share their findings with the class. They found that the Spanish class ate $\frac{1}{3}$ of 4 dozen or $1\frac{1}{3}$ dozen, so they knew that $2\frac{2}{3}$ dozen were left. When they multiplied $\frac{1}{4} \times 2\frac{2}{3}$ to find out how many cookies were left after school, they found that there was $\frac{2}{3}$ of a dozen left. However, they were now "stuck" and unsure if they got the same answer as those who changed 4 dozen to 48 cookies. Miss Stallard asked, "How can we tell if they got the same results?" Elizabeth said that they could multiply $\frac{2}{3} \times 12 = 8$ to see that $\frac{2}{3}$ of a dozen was the same as 8 cookies or $\frac{1}{6}$ of the original cookies.

Through the problem exploration, Miss Stallard led her students to explore the concept of fraction operations. Rather than beginning with a lecture on when to use addition, subtraction, multiplication, and division with fractions, she chose to allow students to gain an understanding of the concept by making sense of the problem in their own ways. Miss Stallard selected a problem task with significant mathematics and allowed students to explore the task and build understanding. She allowed misconceptions, knowing that they are just an expression of students' thinking, but used the misconceptions to question and prompt students to further explore the ideas. She provided many opportunities for math talk, with partners, groups, and the whole class. And she repeatedly asked students to justify their answers. She recorded key ideas on the board to allow all students to see, hear, and think about the key ideas that grew out of the lesson. Through task selection, thoughtful grouping, and frequent prompting and questioning, the teacher was able to lead her students to important insights about operations with fractions in a way that engaged them, stimulated their thinking, and built new math understandings.

Problems as a Teaching Tool

As we become more comfortable allowing students to explore problems even before some skills have been taught, we begin to recognize that students often discover many math ideas on their own. A goal of problem-centered instruction is to pose problems frequently enough to allow students to explore skills, learn to apply skills, and in so doing advance their thinking, arouse their curiosity, and generate insights. Problems are a tool for extending our students' understanding of math.

Problem solving is both a process and a skill. It is a process, a way in which students learn about math ideas. Through problem explorations, students expand their understanding of math concepts and develop their math skills. But problem solving is also a skill to be learned by students. Through the development of some critical problem-solving strategies, which we will explore in the following chapters, students can become more skillful at solving even complex math problems.

CLASSROOM-TESTED TIP

Involving All Students

For group problem-solving tasks, consider ways to organize the experience so that all students in the group become involved in the task. Assigning jobs to group members is a way to engage everyone in the activity. Typical jobs might include leader, reporter, checker, or recorder. Passing out cards to each member with their job designation will remind them of their role. Be sure to explain each job so students will understand their responsibilities. Some typical job descriptions might be:

- The leader reads the problem and makes sure everyone has a chance to speak.

- The reporter shares the group's solution with the class.

- The recorder writes down ideas as the group discusses the task.

■ The checker double-checks the group's work when the students believe they are done.

Assigning jobs does not mean that students each do only a part of the task, as collaboration is critical. The jobs simply organize the task to ensure that all students participate in the problem-solving experience and contribute toward the solution.

Questions for Discussion

1. How is the teacher's role in problem-centered instruction different from his or her role in the traditional drill-and-practice style of teaching math? How is the student's role different?

2. What is the role of teacher questioning in a problem-centered classroom? What is the role of student-to-student talk?

3. How can the teacher ensure that students are actually learning key ideas and concepts? How might teachers guide students to discoveries?

4. What can the teacher do to support students who are having difficulty solving problems?

Guiding Students Through the Problem-Solving Process: Focusing on Strategies

The instructional goal is that students will build an increasing repertoire of strategies, approaches, and familiar problems; it is the problem-solving process that is most important, not just the answer.

—National Council of Teachers of Mathematics,
Curriculum and Evaluation Standards for School Mathematics

Teaching math concepts through a problem-centered approach provides opportunities for our students to discover and refine important math ideas. While some students may intuitively know how to approach the problem tasks, organize their thinking, and select appropriate strategies to find solutions, many others need opportunities to identify and develop their problem-solving skills. Whether we are helping our intuitive problem solvers refine their skills or helping our struggling problem solvers develop their skills, attention to the problem-solving process and key problem-solving strategies is essential.

The Problem-Solving Process

Problem solving is a multi-step task. Successful problem solvers move through a series of steps toward the solution. This does not mean that every student thinks through each step in the same way, but that a process occurs within the heads of problem solvers to help them move through a problem from start to finish. Polya (2004) first identified steps in the problem-solving process, and those steps have been used, discussed, and adapted in numerous problem-solving programs and curricula. Helping students identify these steps helps them view problem solving as a series of actions that leads to the eventual solution. The more proficient our students become with the process, the more quickly and intuitively they may move through these steps; but initially, focusing our students on each step will ensure that they have considered the data, developed a logical plan of action, and carried out the plan in an accurate and reasonable way. The following checklist guides students through the critical steps of the problem-solving process:

Problem-Solving Checklist

> Understand the question.
> Choose a plan.
> Try your plan.
> Check your answer.
> Reflect on what you've done.

Breaking Down the Process

I. Understand the Question

- Ask students to think about the problem and decide what they are being asked to solve. This is an important step in focusing students for the problem-solving task ahead. In this initial step in the problem-solving process, students restate the problem in their own words, explaining what it is asking them to do.

- Students might be asked to work in pairs or groups to determine what the problem is asking them to do. Hearing each other's thoughts will strengthen their skills for understanding problems. And understanding the question leads our students to discussions about the data they believe will be useful in solving the problem.

II. Choose a Plan

- Students must decide *how* to solve the problem. They need to identify a plan or strategy for solving the problem.

- Students will need to identify the known data (the data mentioned in the problem) that will help them solve the problem and will have to determine what to do with the data to get to the solution. Often, more than one strategy can be used to solve a problem.

- Whenever possible, have students predict the answer after they have determined their plan. This will provide them with a benchmark later in the process as they look back to check the reasonableness of their answer.

III. Try Your Plan

- Students use their strategies to attempt to find a solution. Consider allowing students to use calculators to help them focus on the problem-solving process. Often, students' anxiety or confusion regarding the calculations distracts them from the primary objective of the lesson, which relates to their problem-solving skills.

◼ Students may try their plans and find that those plans do not lead to a solution. This is an important realization. Students need to recognize that trying and then eliminating a strategy is okay. Finding a solution does not always happen on the first try. Recognizing that a strategy was unsuccessful and deciding on an alternate strategy are important skills in building effective problem solvers.

IV. Check Your Answer

◼ While checking for arithmetic accuracy is important, it is equally important that students recognize that checking their answers includes checking the reasonableness of the answers. Encourage students to ask themselves questions like, "Does this answer make sense?" "Is something not quite right here?"

◼ Asking students to write a summary sentence that relates their answer to the question will force them to look at the question and their answer together and will often help them detect unreasonable answers. This technique is especially helpful for those students who rush from problem to problem, doing the calculations and never looking back to check for reasonableness.

V. Reflect on What You've Done

◼ Students might be asked to explain how they solved the problem or to justify their solution. They might be asked to share other ways of solving the problem or to reflect on what was easy or hard about the task. This step allows students to process what they've done, and it gives teachers valuable insight into students' thinking.

◼ This critical step supports students in better understanding their own thinking (metacognition). It is the step in which students recognize and verbalize how they solved a problem and why they solved it in that way.

Recording Steps in Solving Problems

As with many skills that are multi-step, showing students how to monitor the problem-solving process through the use of writing as a tool to organize and record their ideas will help them process and remember the steps to solving problems. Following are some ideas for supporting students:

◼ Some students may benefit from the use of a checklist or worksheet (see Figure 2–1) to guide them through the process. The format of students' writing might vary, as illustrated in the varied formats on the CD, but the main components (the steps in the problem-solving process) remain consistent to help students remember important steps to consider when solving problems.

■ Offer students open-ended prompts to guide them through the steps, such as those that follow:

Understand the Question	I (We) need to find out . . .
	I (We) already know . . .
Choose a Plan	To get the answer I (we) could
	I (We) think the answer will be . . .
Try Your Plan	Here is my (our) work . . .
Check Your Answer	My (Our) answer makes sense because . . .
Reflect on What You've Done	I (We) got my (our) answer by . . .
	I (We) had trouble. . . . but I (we) . . .

■ Using modified K-W-L charts (What I *Know*, What I *Want* to Know, What I *Learned*), like the ones on the CD, is another effective way for students to record their ideas as they work through the problem-solving process (see the examples in Figure 2–2). The checklist might be posted in the classroom to support students

---

Problem Solving Worksheet

Understand
Tell the problem in your own words.

Plan
How will you solve the problem?

Try
Show how you solved the problem.

Check
Does your answer make sense? Are your calculations correct?

Reflect
Explain how you solved the problem.
What was easy/hard about solving the problem?

Solving Problems Step-by-Step

1. What's the **Question?**	
What do you want to find out?	What do you already know?

2. Make a **Plan.**	3. **Try** your plan.
What strategy will you use to find the answer? What do you predict the answer might be?	Show your work.

4. **Check** your work.
Does your answer make sense? Are your calculations correct?

5. **Reflect** about solving the problem.
Explain how you got your answer.

Figure 2–1 *Asking students to record their ideas helps them recognize and remember the steps of the problem-solving process.*

Problem-Solving K-W-P-L			
What I **Know**	What I **Want** to Find Out	What I **Plan** to Do	What I **Learned**

Figure 2–2 *Modified K-W-L charts help students organize and record their thinking during problem solving.*

during class discussions or as a resource to which they can refer during independent work. It serves to remind students of the important steps in the problem-solving process.

■ As students become more skilled at the process, a written checklist or worksheet may no longer be needed and may even become frustrating to students who have internalized the problem-solving process and are now focusing their attentions on other problem-solving skills. Our knowledge of our students' abilities, gathered through constant monitoring and assessment, helps us recognize those students who will benefit from a step-by-step approach and those who will be more effective without the structured checklist.

CLASSROOM-TESTED TIP

Modeling Your Thinking

The think-aloud is a valuable tool when teaching problem solving. During a think-aloud, the teacher says aloud what she is thinking while working through the problem. The teacher verbalizes more than the math content; she also verbalizes when she is confused and what she does as a result of the confusion, or verbalizes her insights and discoveries as she observes math data. In a think-aloud, students are able to hear the teacher's thoughts as she analyzes the situation and makes decisions:

> *"Let's see—I know that I have 10 pizzas and each person will get $\frac{2}{3}$ of a pizza. That sounds like a division problem. I want to see how many $\frac{2}{3}$ are in 10."*

or

> *"I predicted that the answer would be 12, but I got 130. Something is not right. It wouldn't make sense for the answer to be 130. I think I'll go back and check my calculations to see if I made a mistake."*

Teachers who are cognizant of common errors can direct their think-alouds to those mistakes.

Helping Students Get "Unstuck"

Students often become stuck when attempting to solve problems. When solutions are not immediately apparent, students can become frustrated and give up. Helping them learn ways to get themselves "unstuck" is an important step in their growth as problem solvers. After problem-solving tasks, encourage students to share the ways they got "unstuck". Students might develop their own list of strategies based on their experiences and the experiences of their classmates. Similar ideas can be shared with parents during a parents' night at school, as shown on the CD, providing them with ideas on how to guide their children through home problem-solving activities. Following are some self-help strategies for getting "unstuck."

Jot Down Ideas

Jot down a plan for how you will be solving the problem. You might list the important information or draw a diagram of the problem to get you started.

Restate the Problem in Your Own Words

Are you unsure how to begin? Reread the problem and then say it in your own words. You need to understand the problem before you can go any further.

Cross Out Unnecessary Information

Is the problem confusing, containing too much data? Reread the problem and cross out the unnecessary data to simplify the problem.

Substitute with Simpler Numbers

Does the problem contain large numbers or fractions or decimals that are confusing you? Substitute simpler numbers for the confusing numbers and then figure out how to solve the problem. Once you know how the problem should be solved, just plug the more complicated numbers back into the problem and repeat the process to solve it.

Take a Break

Are you too frustrated to go on? Take a break for a few minutes. Think about or do something else. Then return to the problem refreshed and ready to begin again.

Use a Manipulative

Use everyday objects (paper clips, toothpicks, pennies) to represent the items in the problem. Act out the problem with the manipulatives.

Talk the Problem Through

Talk out loud to yourself or to someone else. Explain the problem and what you think you should do. Listen to yourself as you talk to see if what you say makes sense.

Think of a Similar Problem

Does this problem remind you of another one that you've solved? How did you solve that one? Try that strategy. Does it work here?

Try a Different Strategy

What you're doing doesn't seem to be working. Try something else. Is there a different strategy that you think might work? Try it and see.

Give Yourself a Pep Talk

Think of a problem you solved by sticking with it. Remember a time when you were frustrated but kept on trying until you found the answer. Remind yourself that you can do it!

Involving Students in Instruction

Teaching problem solving is teaching students to think in an organized manner. It is the process of helping students recognize how logical and productive thinking works. To make thinking visible to our students, we use techniques such as think-alouds, co-operative learning activities, visual demonstrations, and hands-on practice. By transforming thinking from an abstract idea to a visible activity, we keep students engaged in the lessons, strengthen their understanding, and help them gain the skills they need to become more organized thinkers.

It is important that students have opportunities to discuss strategies with one another as they formulate and test ideas about how to proceed with each problem (Whitin and Whitin, 2000). Cooperative-learning strategies are valuable tools during problem-solving instruction, as they allow students to hear each other's thoughts and help each child expand his or her repertoire of ideas. Working with partners or groups gives students the opportunity to test their ideas on others or analyze their teammates' ideas and solutions. Group work helps students monitor their thinking, analyze their progress, and discuss alternate methods of solving each problem. Working with others also helps reduce the anxiety that often comes with "standing alone" and allows students to take risks and gain confidence in their own abilities. It allows them to practice their thinking in a safe and comfortable environment.

Visual and hands-on demonstrations are also critical in helping students understand problem-solving strategies. We might use an overhead projector, video visualizer, blackboard, or erasable board to demonstrate strategies. Using hands-on materials to simulate a problem or create a diagram helps our students see ways to re-create what is happening in the problem. As students develop an understanding of the strategy, the visual and hands-on examples will naturally give way to more abstract thinking.

Students need repeated practice with problem-solving strategies, and they need to be given opportunities to decide which strategies apply to which problems. After providing initial exposure to each strategy, the teacher should give students multiple opportunities to look at a mixed group of problems and determine which strategy makes

Figure 2–3 *Using a calculator allows students to focus on the problem-solving process.*

sense in each situation. Students will often remember certain problems that serve as anchor problems. As students realize, "That's just like the pizza problem!," they will begin to connect the new problem to the familiar "pizza" problem and recognize that applying the same strategy may be successful. During these types of activities, our students need opportunities to hear each other's ideas and discuss the appropriateness of specific strategies, because often more than one strategy may be effective. In the following chapters, we explore the development of problem-solving strategies in greater detail.

A Word About Word Problems

In today's math classrooms, we have expanded and extended our concept of problem solving. Today's word problems strive to push students' thinking with problems that represent more complex situations, require more thinking to find solutions and even may result in multiple answers. They may be short or long, but they always push students to think to find a solution. Some are certainly more complex than others; however, even simple problems can be meaningful and present foundational skills that will later serve our students well as they attempt to solve complex problems. The term *word problems* does not have to be limited to the old-fashioned ones we remember in our textbooks. Problems are in words, because words express ideas and present situations. In equations, the numbers and symbols are written out for us, telling us which operation to use and on which numbers we should be using it. That makes it a rote process. In word problems, the words provide us with a situation and we must decide which data are important, what we are being asked to do, and how we will proceed to find a solution. It is the words that make it challenging and that invite us to think beyond rote. And it is words (discussions and writing) that allow us to teach and explore the problem situations.

The Importance of Problem-Solving Strategies

Problem-solving strategies are what we do in our heads as we make sense of and solve problems. They are our tools for simplifying problems and discovering the possible paths to solutions. Focusing on the development of problem-solving strategies is about helping students understand and employ sound thinking processes, an important goal of mathematics instruction. It is the understanding of these thinking processes, combined with a knowledge of math skills and an understanding of math concepts, that allows our students to effectively solve problems. As our students are challenged to solve problems about fractions, their understanding of the concept of fractions and their knowledge of how to add, subtract, multiply, or divide fractions is important, but without the thinking skills to analyze the problem situation and determine which fractions to use and which operation to apply, students would be unable to find a solution.

Much has been written about the teaching of problem-solving strategies. While there are some variations in the names of the strategies, there is much agreement regarding the critical-thinking skills that play a key role in math problem solving and therefore deserve attention in our math classrooms. The names that have been given to the key problem-solving strategies are simple and are intended to capture the essence of the thinking skills (Choose an Operation; Find a Pattern; Make a Table; Make an Organized List; Draw a Picture or Diagram; Use Logical Reasoning; Guess, Check, and Revise; and Work Backward). Even though the names are quite simple, however, the skills are not. While they can be presented in a simple form to students, these strategies continue to develop in complexity and support students at all grade levels as they attempt to solve even the most complex of problems. Beneath the simple strategy names lies an array of important skills that empowers students to be more effective problem solvers. To sum up, then, the simple problem-solving strategies are not simple at all, but represent significant thinking skills. Students who become adept at using these thinking skills are armed with the tools they need to face many and varied problems.

As we explore problem-solving strategies throughout this book, it is important to remember that we are not teaching or telling students to use a particular strategy, but rather helping them develop the thinking skills to find an appropriate strategy for solving a problem. Often more than one strategy will lead to a solution. Students' work should be evaluated based on the reasonableness of the strategy, not whether it was the strategy we may have had in mind as we posed the problem. Sharing the varied ways that students solve problems enlightens others in the class to possible methods. As we help students recognize and employ varied problem-solving approaches we are helping them build a repertoire of problem-solving strategies, which is the ultimate goal for each of our students (NCTM 1989).

Keys to Developing Strategies

Within a single classroom, students' abilities to understand and apply strategies may differ dramatically. While some students intuitively apply the strategies, others may be at a beginning level in their understanding. These strategies do not develop by grade level, but by experience with and exposure to this type of thinking. Understanding the development of these strategies from simple to complex benefits teachers at all grade levels and provides us with critical knowledge to adjust our instruction. With a deep understanding of these strategies, we are able to break down the skills to support our struggling students or layer on sophistication to challenge our more proficient problem solvers.

Attention to the development of problem-solving strategies should be a component of math instruction at all grade levels. As students move through the grades, these thinking skills are refined and enhanced. The essential thinking skills (e.g., recognizing and extending functional relationships among problem data or working backward using inverse operations to find solutions) are similar, but the tasks become more complicated, requiring additional thought and more complex math skills. Facility with problem-solving strategies does not develop in a single lesson, but rather continues to develop over the years as students experience and explore problems of increasing sophistication. Understanding the progression of these skills, from simple to complex, allows teachers to effectively meet students' needs and to help them refine and extend their understanding of each strategy. As you explore the practice problems on the CD you will notice the increasing complexity within each set of problems and will be able to differentiate lessons by choosing problems based on the needs of your students.

In grades 6 through 8, it is a good practice to introduce each strategy early in the school year. While some students may have seen and discussed the strategies before, others may be seeing them for the first time. Beginning at a simple level will help students experience success and will provide an opportunity to discuss the underlying thinking skills. Visual or hands-on activities are particularly helpful in helping students visualize the strategy.

Once students have been introduced to each strategy, frequent practice tasks provide opportunities for them to revisit the skills. Quality is better than quantity in practice sessions, as we place more emphasis on talking through a few problems than on completing many problems. Questions like, "What strategy did you use to solve that problem?" "How did you know to use that strategy?" and "What was confusing about that problem, and what did you do to make it easier?" should be frequently heard in sixth- through eighth-grade classrooms. Prompting our students to think about similar problems with prompts like, "When have we seen something like this before?" or "Does this problem remind you of any you have done before?" will help them improve their skills in selecting appropriate strategies.

Stimulating communication about these thinking strategies is a key component of developing the skills. Students' metacognitive skills increase as they are challenged to think about and express their own thinking. Students should be frequently asked to explain, justify, and reflect on their problem solving. Prompts like those in Figure 2–4 will push students' thinking.

Through teacher talk and think-alouds, student-to-student discussions about problems, whole-class debriefings after problem solving, and opportunities to write about their insights and experiences, students begin to hear each other's ideas and practice expressing their own. It is during these communication activities that the simple strategy names (e.g., Find a Pattern, Use Logical Reasoning, Work Backward) serve to support our students because they now have words to express the abstract thinking processes they are experiencing.

CLASSROOM-TESTED TIP

Problem-Solving Icons

As students attempt to select an appropriate strategy for solving a problem, the use of icons (pictures to represent the strategies) can serve to remind them of the strategies they have explored in class (see Figure 2–5). A bulletin board or special area of the classroom can be designated to display icons. As students explore a specific strategy, an icon for that strategy is posted. Additional icons are posted as students build their repertoire of strategies. Throughout the year, as students attempt to solve problems, the teacher can direct their attention to the icons as reminders of possible solution strategies. See Strategy Icons on the CD for reproducible icons to post in your classroom or Strategy Bookmarks on the CD for a template to create math bookmarks that display the icons for student reference during class or homework assignments.

Ask students to explain how they solve problems.

- List the steps you used to solve this problem.
- Explain how you solved this problem.
- What might be another way to solve this problem?

Ask students to justify their answers or their decisions.

- Which strategy did you choose? Why do you think that strategy was a good choice for solving this problem?
- Justify why you believe your answer is correct.
- Explain why you set up your (table, diagram, list, etc.) the way you did.

Ask students to write problems of their own.

- Write a problem that can be solved using (multiplication, division, working backward, etc.).
- Write a problem that can be solved by using a table (or finding a pattern or drawing a picture, etc.).
- Write a problem about $10\frac{1}{4} \div 1\frac{1}{2}$.
- Write a problem that requires several steps in order to be solved.

Ask students to reflect on their strengths, weaknesses, and feelings as they learn problem solving.

- What was easy about solving this problem? What was hard?
- What are you still confused about? Do you have any questions that need to be answered?
- Now I understand . . .
- I get frustrated when . . .
- When I don't know what to do I . . .
- I discovered that . . .
- Next time I will . . .

Figure 2–4 *Talking and Writing About Problem Solving*

Figure 2–5 *Icons posted in the classroom remind students of possible strategies for solving math problems.*

Exploring the Strategies in Detail

While most textbooks and curricula contain problems focused on these strategies, assigning these problem tasks will not teach these skills. It is the selection of problems combined with discussion, exploration, and reflection that supports students as they develop an understanding of problem-solving strategies. Although we were all assigned problems, we were not all taught how to solve math problems. It is the way in which we explore and illustrate the strategies that is most important to the development of our students' skills. In the following chapters, we will explore each strategy in more detail. We will look at visual, hands-on, and interactive ways to present, explore, and discuss a variety of problem-solving strategies so that students will be able to understand and apply the strategies to make sense of and solve a wide range of math problems.

Questions for Discussion

1. In what ways can students benefit from understanding their own thinking (metacognition) as they solve problems? How can we support them in recognizing both the process and strategies that they use to solve problems?

2. Why is it important to help students build a repertoire of strategies?

3. What is the role of communication (talk and writing) in developing problem-solving strategies?

4. Why might it be important for a teacher to understand the progression of skills in these problem-solving strategies?

5. Many students get stuck during their attempts to solve problems. What tips for getting "unstuck" might be helpful to them? How might these ideas be shared?

CHAPTER 3

Strategy: Choose an Operation

Understanding the fundamental operations of addition, subtraction, multiplication, and division is central to knowing mathematics. One essential component of what it means to understand an operation is recognizing conditions in real-world situations that indicate that the operation would be useful in those situations.

—National Council of Teachers of Mathematics,
Curriculum and Evaluation Standards for School Mathematics

We acknowledge the importance of helping students understand the problem-solving process, the way to proceed through a problem from start to finish. We recognize that students must be able to identify the question or determine what they are being asked to find out before they can effectively find a solution. But we also recognize that once students know what they are being asked to solve, they must be able to consider varied approaches and decide on a plan that makes sense for that problem. Choosing an operation (addition, subtraction, multiplication, or division) is a method for solving many math problems. Determining which operation is appropriate for solving a problem is a critical, and frequently used, problem-solving strategy.

Students' ability to select the correct operation when solving word problems often reflects the way in which they were taught each operation. Students who memorized math facts without developing a clear understanding of the concepts may have more difficulty identifying when to use each operation than students who developed an understanding of each concept through demonstrations, explanations, and hands-on experiences. Students in the middle grades who are struggling with problem solving may need to revisit the concept of when to use each operation. When talking about multiplication, for example, it is important that students see and hear situations in which groups of equal size are joined. After repeatedly experiencing the concept, students are able to understand the operation involved in 3 × 4, rather than just knowing that the answer is 12 because of repeated flash card practice.

Key Words Versus Key Concepts

Even though teachers often use key words as a method of assisting students in choosing an appropriate operation, be careful about teaching students to rely solely on key words (Sowder 2002). It is often true that when the word *altogether* appears in a problem, it is an addition problem. Those words, however, can appear in other problems, and students who look for one or two familiar words but do not stop to analyze the entire problem may incorrectly determine that addition is the operation to use. Consider the following problem:

> **Terrance and his sister shared a pizza. They ate $\frac{5}{8}$ of the pizza altogether. If Terrance ate $\frac{1}{4}$ of the pizza, how much did his sister eat?**

While the word *altogether* does appear, it is not an indication of the correct operation as this is actually a subtraction problem. Particularly with the increase in real-world problem-solving tasks and more complex performance tasks, there may be several key words within a problem that will mislead the student who is relying only on key words.

Students should look for key concepts rather than key words. After reading the problem, they should visualize the situation rather than focusing on a word or phrase in hopes that it will tell them how to proceed. Understanding the key concepts for each operation will help students make a thoughtful decision regarding the appropriate operation to use in solving the problem.

Practice with Recognizing Key Concepts

It is important that our students learn how to add, subtract, multiply, and divide, but to be effective problem solvers our students also need to recognize *when* to perform each operation. Understanding math operations is more than simply knowing how to perform calculations; it is understanding when each operation makes sense to solve a problem. It is critical that students understand the concepts of addition, subtraction, multiplication, and division.

Addition

Students in the elementary grades explore addition as a process of bringing groups together or joining parts to create a whole. Elementary school teachers help students understand addition as they place groups of objects on the overhead and physically pull them together or provide students with desktop manipulatives to illustrate basic addition problems. By grades 6 to 8, students should have a good understanding of addition; however, as numbers become more complex (e.g., fractions, decimals, large numbers), students still benefit greatly from hands-on experiences and visual demonstrations to extend their understanding of the operation of addition (as well as the other operations). Using fraction pieces to demonstrate addition of fractions or allowing students to explore with base-ten blocks as they develop an understanding of adding decimals will help them better understand the concept of addition.

Subtraction

While addition is about finding the whole by joining the parts, subtraction focuses on finding a missing part. Starting with the whole and removing a part is the traditional *take-away* model. If there were 50 pieces of candy in a bag and we ate 13 of them, subtraction would help us find out how many pieces of candy remain in the bag.

Another significant model for subtraction is the *compare* model. When items are compared, we use subtraction to find the difference between them. If we are asking students to determine how much one object is taller, wider, or heavier than another, they would subtract to find the difference. However, students must be careful. Not every problem involving comparison uses subtraction. For example, consider the following problem:

Miguel has 16 more CDs than Jana. If Jana has 37 CDs, how many CDs does Miguel have?

Although this problem involves a comparison, students would need to use addition to solve it. Miguel's 16 additional CDs must be added to Jana's 37 CDs in order to find the solution. In this case, we are not finding the *difference* between the number of CDs each student has, but are using a comparison to find Miguel's *total* number of CDs.

In the following comparison problem, students are finding how many CDs must be added to Jana's 37 to reach 53, or $37 + \square = 53$, so using subtraction makes sense.

If Miguel has 53 CDs and Jana has 37 CDs, how many more CDs would Jana need to buy to have the same amount as Miguel?

Subtracting Jana's 37 CDs from the 53 that Miguel has will result in the difference between them.

Multiplication

Like addition, multiplication is used to find the total number of objects; however, when using multiplication, all sets must have the same number of objects. If there are 6 cartons of milk and each carton has $\frac{1}{2}$ gallon in it, multiplication can be used to find the total number of gallons of milk. Using manipulatives (e.g., cubes or counters) to represent multiplication scenarios, constructing arrays to model situations, and posing real-world multiplication problems help students continue to experience the concept of multiplication.

As middle grades students encounter problems involving multiplication of fractions and decimals, the concept of multiplication becomes a bit more complex. Consider the following problem:

> **Shelley and her sister found $\frac{3}{4}$ of a pizza in the refrigerator. Shelley's sister told Shelley that she wanted $\frac{1}{2}$ of the remaining pizza. If Shelley gives her sister what she wants, how much pizza will Shelley have left?**

Many students may think that Shelley will have $\frac{1}{4}$ of the original pizza left. They may view this as a subtraction problem rather than a multiplication problem and give Shelley's sister $\frac{1}{2}$ of a whole pizza rather than $\frac{1}{2}$ of the remaining pizza. It is important to help them understand that Shelley's sister wants $\frac{1}{2}$ of $\frac{3}{4}$ of 1 whole pizza, which means $\frac{1}{2} \times \frac{3}{4}$ or $\frac{3}{8}$ of a whole pizza. Using manipulatives, drawing pictures (see Figure 3–1), and engaging students in discussions about the problem scenario will help them understand why they should multiply rather than subtract. And asking students to predict reasonable answers prior to doing computations will help them recognize errors in their work.

Division

Understanding that division is the inverse of multiplication helps students see division as a search for missing factors. Division is often seen as fair sharing or partitioning. The quotient might represent the number of groups that are formed or the number of items in each group. While the groups that are formed have equal quantities, it is important that students understand that remainders may result. And it is important for students in grades 6 to 8 to connect fractions and division, understanding that $\frac{2}{3}$ represents 2 divided by 3.

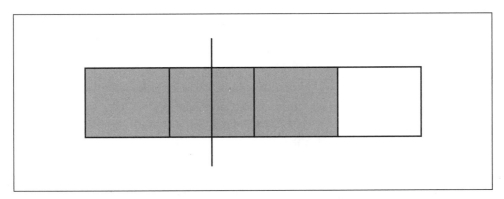

Figure 3–1 *If the rectangle represents one whole pizza, this diagram shows $\frac{1}{2}$ of $\frac{3}{4}$ of 1 whole pizza.*

Division can be especially confusing when dealing with fractions or decimals. Consider the following problem:

> **Demarcus has 3.25 pounds of candy. He wants to make small bags of 0.35 pounds each to share with his friends. How many friends will receive a bag of candy from Demarcus if he keeps one bag for himself?**

In this problem, students must divide 3.25, which represents the whole amount of candy, by 0.35, which is the size of the smaller groups being formed. Students will see that the result of the division indicates that Demarcus can keep one bag of candy and still share 8 more bags. Students can talk about what the remainder means. If they imagine themselves in his place, they may conclude that the remainder represents extra candy for Demarcus to keep!

A confusing aspect of dividing by fractions or decimals with a value less than one is that the quotient becomes greater than the dividend. Helping students understand this fact will help them better identify when their answers are reasonable. If Demarcus has 10 pounds of candy and divides it into 5-pound bags, he will get 2 bags (a quotient less than the original 10 pounds of candy, the dividend). If he has 10 pounds of candy and divides it into 1-pound bags, he will get 10 bags (a quotient the same as the original number of pounds of candy). If he has 10 pounds of candy and divides it into 0.5 or $\frac{1}{2}$-pound bags, he will get 20 bags of candy (a quotient greater than the number of pounds he started with). And that makes sense because the original amount, the dividend, is being divided into groups less than one. Sharing some examples, through word problems or class demonstrations, to help students see the relationships between the dividends and the quotients may help them better understand division by fractions and decimals.

Practice with Choosing the Correct Operation

Group Activities and Discussions

It is important for students to have opportunities to practice selecting the appropriate operation. This can be done through pair and group activities in which students are given a team problem and asked to determine the correct operation. As students discuss which operation they would choose and why, they are able to hear each other's ideas and strengthen their understanding of the key concepts. When sharing their answers with the rest of the class, students should always include a justification for their choice of operations, telling why they chose the operation they did.

Pinch Cards

Pinch cards, a form of all-pupil response, also provide practice in identifying the correct operation. All students receive their own card. Teachers can create their own cards, being sure to duplicate the operation signs on both sides of the cards, or use the Pinch Cards samples on the CD. The operation signs should be placed in the same location on the front and back of the card, so students can see the sign from the back of the card while teachers see the same sign from the front. As the teacher poses a problem, students pinch (hold the card by that sign) the operation they would use to solve the problem. The teacher then briefly asks students to justify their decisions. This allows a quick, interactive review that students enjoy, and it allows teachers to quickly spot those students who are still having difficulty with the concepts. Those students may be pulled aside later for review or reteaching.

Student-Created Problems

Asking students to develop their own problems related to sets of data is another way to help them strengthen their understanding of math operations. Give students a set of data and ask them to create a real problem that might use the data. For example, students may write a variety of problems using the following data.

Data: **6 hamburgers, $1.95 per hamburger, 4 people**

Sample student-created problems include:

"There were 6 hamburgers and 4 people. If they shared equally, how many hamburgers would each person get?"
"Four people bought 6 hamburgers. Each hamburger costs $1.95. How much did each of them spend?"
"Three people had $1\frac{1}{4}$ hamburgers each. The other person ate the rest. How many hamburgers did he eat?"
"One person bought two hamburgers and paid with a $5.00 bill. How much change did she get back?"
"Christopher had $6.00. How many hamburgers could he buy?"

After students write their story problems, have them present the problems to their group or to the entire class. Students might trade problems between partners or groups and solve each other's problems. Students can be asked to sort the problems by operation. Some of the student-written problems might be used for class problem-solving warm-ups over the next few days. Asking students to explain how they knew which operation they should use to solve each problem is a critical part of the thinking process.

CLASSROOM-TESTED TIP

Writing Word Problems

Using equations to prompt students to write word problems is an effective way to assess students' understanding of the basic operations. Provide students with an equation and ask them to create a word problem to match the equation. Consider the following equation: $0.25 \times \$23.80 = \$5.95$.

Story: *Samantha bought a blouse that usually costs $23.80. However, everything in the store was marked down 25% that day. How much did Samantha save on her blouse?*

Here is another story that might go with the same equation:

Brandon and his brother ate lunch at a local restaurant. The total amount that they spent for their food was $23.80. How much more will they have to pay if the sales tax rate is 7% and they want to leave a tip of 18%?

Writing word problems from equations can be challenging. Allowing students to work with a partner or group provides support for students who are having difficulty creating problems on their own. Students can record their problems in math journals or share their group problems aloud with the whole class. Classmates can evaluate each problem and use a thumbs-up response to confirm that the problem matches the equation. If problems don't match the equation, classmates can suggest ways to rewrite the problem to make it fit. Writing word problems helps students strengthen their understanding of operations.

A variation of this activity is to pair up students and give each student a different equation on an index card. Ask students to turn over their index card so their partner cannot see it, then write a word problem for their equation. When students have finished, have them switch index cards with their partner. After reading their partner's problem, students must figure out the related equation.

Focusing on Increasingly Complex Problems

The complexity of math problems increases in grades 6 through 8, and helping students understand and solve more complex problems becomes an important component of problem-solving instruction. Rather than being asked to solve the simple one- and two-step problems that were posed in the elementary grades, students in the middle grades are faced with problems that may be multi-step, require students to select appropriate data from a set of data, or to convert data in order to find solutions. Exploring ways in which problems become more complex, and helping our students recognize and solve these problems is an important role of the middle-grades mathematics teacher.

During the middle grades, students are often faced with finding the data they need to solve a problem. Sometimes unnecessary data are presented in the problem and students must determine what is needed and what is not needed to find a solution. The following problem contains unnecessary information:

The students in Mr. Gorin's homeroom donated cupcakes and brownies to sell at the school bake sale. There are 32 students in Mr. Gorin's homeroom. Cup-

cakes were sold for $0.65 each and brownies were sold for $0.50 each. They sold 192 cupcakes and 256 brownies. How much money did they make?

Students do not need to know that there are 32 students in Mr. Gorin's homeroom, and yet that information appears in the problem and often confuses students who are unsure of which data to use. The ability to identify unnecessary information is a critical problem-solving skill. Students need to be able to understand the question being asked and to identify the data that specifically address that question. Focusing on identifying unnecessary information is essentially focusing on whether students *know the question* and *know the data needed to find an answer*. Asking students to state what they are trying to find out and what they already know helps them to focus on the connection between the data and the question. Teachers might ask students to cross out unnecessary data in the problem. Asking them to clarify why the information is not needed helps ensure their understanding. Breanna said that she did not need to know that there were 32 students in Mr. Gorin's homeroom. When asked to explain why that information was unnecessary, she stated, "because I only needed to know how many cupcakes and brownies were sold to find out how much money they made, not how many people donated cupcakes and brownies." Breanna understood what she was being asked to solve and was able to identify the data that would get her to a solution.

Problems in grades 6 through 8 often provide students with a bank of data from which to choose. Consider the problem that asks students to determine how much a mix of $1\frac{1}{2}$ pounds each of gum drops, peppermints, and caramels would cost. Students need to use the Sue's Candy Store price list to locate the appropriate data and then use that information to solve the problem.

Sue's Candy Store Pricelist

> Jelly Beans $59.90 / 10 lbs.
> Gum Drops $23.95 / 8 lbs.
> Caramels $47.93 / 7.5 lbs.
> Chocolate Mints $37.60 / 6 lbs.
> Peppermints $27.93 / 7 lbs.
> Peanut Butter Cups $39.90 / 5 lbs.
> Toffee $32.37 / 10 lbs.

Students must now select the needed data from a set of data and then know how to proceed to solve the problem. Understanding that they must find the price per pound (divide) for the gum drops, peppermints, and caramels, then find the price (multiply) for $1\frac{1}{2}$ pounds of each, then combine (add) all three prices, requires students to select appropriate data, understand operations, and perform multi-step tasks.

In multi-step problems, students are required to interpret and solve a problem that has multiple components. Students might be asked to solve the following problem:

Steffi and Amanda are making costumes from their favorite video game. Steffi bought $2\frac{3}{4}$ yards of fabric that cost $5.75 per yard, and Amanda bought $3\frac{5}{8}$ yards

of fabric that cost $6.99 per yard. If they pay for the fabric with a $50.00 bill, how much change will they get back?

Students must apply a variety of skills in order to successfully solve multi-step problems. Rather than looking at a simple problem in which they may have recognized the operation of addition and added the only two numbers within the problem, they now need to identify significant data, know what to do with that information, and understand and proceed through a series of steps that lead to a solution. In the previous problem, students might multipy the price per yard by the quantity to find the cost of Steffi's fabric, then do the same to find the cost of Amanda's fabric. They must then add to find the total cost of the fabric. But even then they are not done, because they need to subtract the total from $50.00 to determine how much change Steffi and Amanda will receive.

In helping students understand and effectively solve multi-step tasks like this one, teachers might first split the task into parts so that students can find the first solution and then move on to the next step. This helps some students gain confidence as well as develop their understanding of the multi-step process. Teachers also might ask students to circle or underline the questions being asked in a problem, reminding them that the problem may include more than one question. And providing opportunities for students to discuss and write about the steps they took to solve more complex problems is critical.

Math problems in the middle grades also are often complicated with conversions. Examples of conversion problems are provided below:

Josh had a square garden. Each side measured 9 feet. What was the area in yards?

Jenna baked cookies for the sixth-grade party. There were 81 students in the sixth grade. How many dozen cookies did she need to bake so that every sixth-grade student could have at least 1 cookie?

In each case, students need to understand the question and how the question data differ from the data being asked for in the solution (i.e., feet vs. yards, individual cookies vs. dozen). They also need the computation skills to convert their answers into yards or dozens. Understanding the measurements and determining how to make the conversions adds to the complexity of the tasks, but isn't that what we hope our students will be able to do: to use their math skills to think through increasingly complex situations? We have lofty goals in problem solving and can become frustrated when our students' thinking doesn't progress quickly, but remembering the importance of teaching problem solving helps us stay focused on modeling good thinking and supporting our students as they struggle to develop their thinking skills. Continually asking "What do we need to find out?" "What do we know?" "How will the data help us?" "What steps will we need to take to find the solution?" and "Does our answer match the question?" will continue to focus students on key questions to drive their problem-solving experiences.

Frequent talk about methods for approaching multi-step tasks will help bolster student understanding. Highlighting the steps needed to find the solution will focus attention on the multi-step aspect. We might ask students what should be done first to get us started, or what else we need to figure out in order to continue working toward a solution. Having students work with partners to explore multi-step tasks will encourage communication, pushing students to talk about their thinking and share their strategies for moving through the multiple tasks. And frequent and specific feedback on their efforts will provide students with insight into where they might be going off-track or ways in which their hard work and reflection have increased their problem-solving abilities.

CLASSROOM-TESTED TIP

Simplifying Problems

In grades 6 through 8, problems become more complicated for students as the math data are increasingly sophisticated. As fractions, money, decimals, or large numbers appear in problems, students may become anxious and confused about how to solve the problem. Show students how to substitute simpler numbers into the problem and then discuss how they might solve the simpler problem. Often students are better able to assess the problem when they are not overwhelmed by the data. Consider this problem:

> **Sarah had some ribbon to make bows. Anna gave her $10\frac{2}{3}$ yards of additional ribbon. Now Sarah has $26\frac{1}{6}$ yards of ribbon. How many yards of ribbon did Sarah have at the beginning?**

Students might replace the mixed numbers with simple whole numbers and then determine their plan for solving the problem.

> **Sarah had some ribbon to make bows. Anna gave her 3 yards of additional ribbon. Now Sarah has 5 yards of ribbon. How many yards of ribbon did Sarah have at the beginning?**

Using simpler data allows students to see the problem more clearly. Once they have recognized that subtraction is a plan for finding the solution, they can go back to the original problem and replace and then subtract the mixed numbers. Teaching students strategies for simplifying problems is an important goal of problem-solving instruction.

Communicating About the Strategy

Asking students to talk and write about how and why they arrived at an answer or selected an operation helps teachers better assess their understanding of the operations. Allowing students to work in pairs or groups to discuss their choice of operations will help them develop ways to verbalize their thoughts. By listening to others and sharing ideas, they begin to acquire the vocabulary they need to explain their mathematical thinking. It is important to encourage students to put their thoughts in writing to help them process their understanding and help us better assess their knowledge. In Figure 3–2, the student shows her work and explains the multi-step process she used to find the answer. Even those students who may require the use of pictures or diagrams to support their explanations will benefit from attempts to explain their thinking.

Candy Mix

The sixth grade is planning their end-of-the-year party, and they want to make a batch of candy mix. They will need $2\frac{1}{2}$ pounds of each candy.

Cost of Candy

Jelly Beans – $39.90/10 lb.
Chocolate Covered Raisins – $44.92/7.5 lb.
Candy Covered Peanuts – $48.95/10 lb.

How much will the candy mix cost? $\underline{\$\ 37.21}$

Show your work.
$39.90 \div 10 = 3.99$ each lb.
$44.92 \div 7.5 = 5.99$ each lb.
$48.95 \div 10 = 4.90$ each lb.

$3.99 \times 2.5 = 9.98$
$5.99 \times 2.5 = 14.98$
$4.90 \times 2.5 = 12.25$
$\overline{\text{total} = 37.21}$

List the steps you took to solve the problem.

I took 39.90 divided by 10 and did that to every type of candy. And then I got how much each lb. is and multiplied it by how many lbs. we needed. then I added the answers to get the final total.

Figure 3–2 *This student explains the steps she took to solve this multi-step task.*

Following are some discussion or writing prompts to extend students' thinking about operations:

- What operation did you use to solve this problem? Why?

- Explain the steps you used to solve this problem.

- Justify your answer.

- How did you decide on the equation you used to solve this problem? Would another equation have worked also?

Selecting Practice Problems

Practice problems using addition, subtraction, multiplication, and division are available in any math book. Students need practice with identifying operations and building appropriate equations to represent problem situations. And continuing to increase the complexity of the problem tasks through multi-step problems or problems with unnecessary information will help develop and refine their problem-solving skills. While these problems can be found in textbooks, keep in mind that real-world problems that connect math to events and situations in students' lives will motivate and excite them. Simple activities like rewording textbook problems to include your students' names or the names of local restaurants, parks, or schools will help to personalize the problem-solving experience. The practice problems provided on the accompanying CD can be modified on your computer prior to printing them. Add your students' names or the names of local businesses and attractions. In addition, using data from local menus, travel brochures, or baseball cards will keep students involved in your lessons and demonstrate the meaningfulness of the mathematics skills they are learning. Seize any opportunity to make a real-world connection for your students.

Questions for Discussion

1. Why is it important for students to understand the operations?

2. What is the difference between key words and key concepts?

3. How can visual and hands-on activities support students' understanding of operations?

4. What are the difficulties associated with multi-step problems? How might teachers support students as problems become more complex?

CHAPTER 4

Strategy: Find a Pattern

By continuing to provide a broad variety of opportunities to explore and use patterns, we help students move from a basic recognition of patterns to a more sophisticated use of patterns as a problem-solving strategy.

—Terrence G. Coburn, NCTM *Addenda Series—Patterns*

Patterns are central to our number system. Students begin to recognize and repeat patterns early in their mathematics education, and these patterns become more complicated by the time students reach the middle grades. This ability to understand, identify, and extend patterns helps students solve many math problems.

Patterns range from simple to very complex. Students in the primary grades become adept at pattern recognition, begin to internalize the concept that patterns repeat in a predictable way, and learn to extend them. As students progress through school the patterns become increasingly sophisticated and require them to observe carefully and draw conclusions about their observations. Students in grades 6 to 8 should be provided with opportunities to explore a variety of patterns in our number system as well as patterns in geometry and other areas of mathematics. Middle grades students should be guided to appreciate the power of patterns in solving problems, as it is often through the discovery of a pattern that students are able to progress toward a solution to a problem.

Completing and Describing Number Patterns

Patterns are everywhere in our number system. We begin by introducing simple patterns and challenging students with increasingly complex number patterns to help them develop a greater understanding of numbers and operations. While many math activities ask students to simply complete a pattern, asking our students to describe patterns extends their thinking and helps us better analyze their understandings. Students describe their understanding of a variety of number patterns below:

3, 6, 12, 24 . . .
"You doubled the number each time."

2, 3, 5, 9, 17 . . .
"First you added one, then two, then four, then eight."

5, 2, –1, -4 . . .
"I subtracted three each time."

1, 4, 9, 16, 25 . . .
"I multiplied 1 × 1, then 2 × 2, then 3 × 3, then 4 × 4, then 5 × 5."

When asking students to describe patterns, ask for multiple responses. Patterns can accurately be described in a variety of ways, and allowing students to hear different ways helps them to bridge ideas about various operations and better understand the patterns. When describing the pattern 7, 14, 21, 28 . . . , students might say:

"I skip-counted by sevens."
"I said all of the multiples of 7."
"I added 7 to each number."

Each student has accurately described the pattern. Together, their descriptions show connections between operations and illustrate important understandings about numbers. Asking students to take a closer look at patterns and to describe the patterns that they see can lead them to interesting, and often unexpected, insights. When asked to describe the pattern 4, 8, 12, 16, 20, 24, 28, 32 . . . , students responded:

"It's like counting by fours."
"It's the answers when you multiply 4 × 1, 4 × 2, 4 × 3, 4 × 4 . . . "
"It's like adding 4 to the one before it."
"Hey, first they end with a 4, then 8, then 2, then 6, then 0, then it does it again!"
   (An interesting insight!)

The more we ask students to look for patterns within our number system, the more patterns they will discover!

Pattern Cover-Up

Students can explore patterns through an interactive classroom activity in which they determine missing numbers in a pattern. Write a number pattern on the blackboard, chart paper, or overhead projector. Cover each of the numbers in the sequence with sticky notes (a pattern with five numbers works well). The goal is for students to try to predict the number that is under the last sticky note. Remove one sticky note (any except the last one), asking students to predict and record the sequence hidden under the sticky notes. Then let students share and justify their thoughts on what the last number is by stating the five numbers and describing the pattern: e.g., ___, ___, 30, ___, ___. One student might predict 50 as the final number stating that the pattern is counting by tens: 10, 20, 30, 40, *50*. Another student might predict 40, predicting multiples of 5 starting at 20: 20, 25, 30, 35, *40*. Still another might predict that 10 is the final number as he describes the pattern as subtracting 10 each time beginning with 50: 50, 40, 30, 20, *10*.

After several students have had a chance to share and discuss their predictions, remove another sticky note and ask students to readjust their predictions. Will their final number still work or have they changed their idea of what the pattern might be? Again, have students record their predictions and then have them share with the class or with a partner.

e.g., 25, ___, 30, ___, ___

Now none of the patterns listed would still work. Students will need to consider more complicated possibilities, including decimals or mixed numbers. Continue to remove sticky notes and discuss predictions until the pattern is revealed.

Tip: Support struggling students by providing them with hundred charts to use as a visual as they think about possible patterns.

Making Patterns Visual

While some students have an inate ability to recognize even abstract patterns, other students are greatly supported when they are helped to visualize patterns. Visual tools like number lines or hundred charts help students see and recognize patterns. Even listing and circling numbers is a simple way to help students visualize a pattern. While students might have difficulty recognizing the pattern 5, 2, –1, –4 . . . , seeing it on a number line can bring about an immediate recognition for students who learn best with visual support.

This visual allows students to see that two numbers are skipped each time. Moving patterns from abstract to visual is a significant tool for many of our students.

Working with Geometric Patterns

As students study shapes and chart sides and angles, they will begin to recognize geometic patterns. Take, for example, the following diagonal problem:

Can you predict how many diagonals can be made in an eight-sided figure?

Students can solve the problem by creating the figure and drawing the diagonals, but they can also solve the problem with an understanding of patterns. After students have drawn a few shapes and counted the diagonals, they will be able to predict the number of diagonals for the remaining shapes based on the pattern they have discovered.

Sides	4	5	6	7
Diagonals	2	5	9	14

"I see a pattern. First you added three, then you added four, then you added five. I think you add one more each time. So I would add six this time. My answer is 20 diagonals."

As drawing the figures becomes more difficult, say in the case of an eighteen-sided figure, the use of patterns becomes the preferred—and simpler—way to solve the problem.

Patterns as a Problem-Solving Strategy

Once students become sensitive to searching for patterns, they are able to recognize them in problem situations. The patterns they find give them plans for finding solutions—simply continue patterns to find solutions. This problem shows a simple pattern embedded in a problem task:

Alexis wanted to rent some DVDs for her slumber party. One store offered one DVD for $3.50, two for $7.00, three for $10.50, four for $14.00, and so on. How much did Alexis pay for seven DVDs?

DVDs for Alexis

Alexis wanted to rent some DVDs for her slumber party. She found a store that rented one DVD for $4.00, two for $7.80, three for $11.40, four for $14.80, and so on. Use the pattern to help you figure out how much Alexis would have to pay for seven DVDs.

# of DVD's	Cost
1	$4.00
2	$7.80
3	$11.40
4	$14.80
5	$18.00
6	$21.00
7	$23.80

(margin notations: 80, 60, 40, 20, 00, 80)

Alexis paid ___23.80___ to rent seven DVDs.

Describe the pattern in the problem. The pattern in the problem is that you start from $3.80 and add it on to the cost for one DVD to get the second. Then you subtract .20 from $3.80 then add it to the second and get the price for 3 DVD's then you subtract .20 from $3.60 and get the price for 4 DVD's. Then you keep doing the same thing until you get the price for 7 DVD's.

How did knowing the pattern help you figure out the answer?
Knowing the pattern helps me figure out the awnser because it lets me know what I need to do to get the price for the items I'm buying.

Figure 4–1 *This student used a table to help her identify and describe the pattern in the problem.*

Once the pattern is recognized (3.5, 7, 10.5, 14 . . .), students can continue it to the seventh place to find the solution. But as always, our goal is to continue to challenge students with problems of increasing complexity. This second part of the problem requires understanding a pattern that is less apparent:

> **Alexis found another store that rented one DVD for $4.00, two for $7.80, three for $11.40, four for $14.80, and so on. How much would Alexis have to pay for seven DVDs?**

Students now have to recognize that the price per DVD is changing according to a pattern (4.00, 3.80, 3.60, 3.40 . . .) and again extend it to the seventh place to find the solution. Pattern problems continue to get more complex when patterns merely provide data with which students must solve the problem, as in the following example:

> **The school band members are planning their annual car wash. They looked at the car wash records from the past three years in order to estimate how much they**

could expect to earn. They found that the average amount earned during the first hour was $26.00. An average of $35.35 was taken in during the second hour, and an average of $44.70 was earned during the third hour. During the fourth hour, an average of $54.05 was collected. They noticed that this pattern continued throughout the day. Based on these findings, how much can they expect to earn if the car wash is held from 10:00 a.m. to 4:00 p.m.?

Now the recognition and extension of the pattern merely provides the data needed for solving the problem. Students still must use their understanding of operations, their computational skills, and their knowledge of elapsed time to complete the task. Patterns become one piece—although a critical piece—to solving the problem.

CLASSROOM-TESTED TIP

Finding Mathematicians' Patterns

Show students the first few terms of the following sequence, which is known as the Fibonacci sequence:

0, 1, 1, 2, 3, 5, 8, . . .

In pairs, have students investigate and describe the pattern that they see. Ask them to predict the next few terms based on the pattern they observe. The Fibonacci sequence, where each successive term is the sum of the previous two terms, occurs in a variety of situations in nature, inlcuding the spiral of a nautilus sea shell, petals of flowers, leaves of plants, and the family tree of a male bee. Students can then examine Pascal's Triangle (Figure 4–2), looking for patterns and describing them. In Pascal's triangle, each term other than the first and last of each row is the sum of the two diagonally above it. Both the Fibonacci sequence and Pascal's triangle have interesting and somewhat complex patterns. Pascal's triangle has many applications in mathematics, including its usefulness in calculating probabilities and in determining coefficients for polynomials using the Binomial Theorem. These activities could also lead to discussions about famous mathematicians and their work.

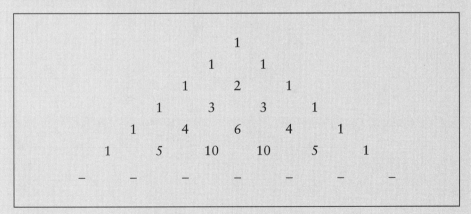

Figure 4–2 *Pascal's Triangle*

Communicating About the Strategy

Asking students to write or talk about creating or extending patterns is a great way to extend their thinking and assess their understanding of patterns. Try prompts like these:

■ Describe the pattern.

■ Explain how understanding patterns helped you solve this problem.

■ Is solving problems using patterns easy or hard? Explain your answer.

■ How did an understanding of patterns help you find the data you needed to solve the problem?

■ If a new student entered the room who did not know anything about patterns, how would you explain what they are and how they can help you solve problems? Give an example to help them understand.

Questions for Discussion

1. How does an understanding of patterns help students have a better grasp of place value and operations?

2. How can an understanding of patterns help students solve problems?

3. How might teachers support students who have trouble recognizing patterns?

4. In what ways can an understanding of patterns support students who are struggling with basic math facts?

Strategy: Make a Table

Organizing data in a table is an essential mathematical skill. It helps children to see relationships within patterns and eventually to generalize these relationships to form a rule.

—Terrence G. Coburn, NCTM *Addenda Series—Patterns*

The ability to organize data so that it can be used to solve problems is a critical skill. Tables are one way students can organize data in order to see the data more clearly, recognize patterns and relationships within the data, and gain insights about missing data. When making tables, students are challenged to put important problem data in an organized form.

When focusing on the development of this strategy, there are several critical points to address. Students need to understand how to create a table, including which items to list in the table, where to record specific data in the table, how to determine when enough information has been gathered to complete the table, and even how to select the correct answer from the many numbers that are recorded in the table. Students must acquire the skill of recognizing and extending patterns and identifying functional relationships in order to construct and interpret tables accurately. And of course, recognizing whether creating a table makes sense for a problem is a critical skill. Spending time addressing each of these issues ensures that students have a solid understanding of this strategy.

Using Tables to Solve Problems

Tables are helpful in showing relationships between data. Take the following data, for example: *At the bake sale, each brownie costs $0.85.* A table like the one that follows can help students find out the cost for 2, 3, 4, or 5 brownies. In this problem, there is a relationship—a connection—between the cost of each brownie and the number of brownies, and the table shows that relationship. Every brownie costs $0.85, so each time a brownie is added to the top row of the table, $0.85 must be added to the corresponding column on the bottom row. By creating a table, students are able to get a better look at the data, use patterns to explore the data, and use the data to solve problems.

Number of boxes	1	2	3	4	5
Cost of brownies	$0.85	$1.70	$2.55	$3.40	$4.25

To use tables as an effective problem-solving strategy, students must be able to recognize times when creating a table could help identify solutions. A critical insight in deciding if a table might be an appropriate strategy is recognizing two (or more) items in the problem that have a relationship or a connection, meaning that one item is connected to the other in a predictable way. Teacher modeling, through think-alouds, is an effective way to start discussions and exploration of the appropriate use of tables as a problem-solving strategy. Take the following problem:

To make 1 batch of chocolate chip cookies, I need $1\frac{3}{4}$ cups of flour. If I have 7 cups of flour, how many batches of cookies can I make?

What do we already know? There is a relationship, a connection, between the amount of flour and the number of cookie batches. Can we figure out how many cups of flour we would need for batches based on what we know? How about 3 batches? If I make 1 batch, then I need $1\frac{3}{4}$ cups of flour. So, if I make 2 batches, then I need [$1\frac{3}{4} + 1\frac{3}{4}$] or $3\frac{1}{2}$ cups of flour. If I make 3 batches, I need [$1\frac{3}{4} + 1\frac{3}{4} + 1\frac{3}{4}$] or $5\frac{1}{4}$ cups of flour, and so on. How can we display that data so we can see it more clearly? How about a table on which we can record the data as we figure it out? We can help students build their understanding by talking them through the creation of the table, asking questions such as these, and including discussions about our thinking and the decisions we make as we move toward a solution.

To help students develop this skill, we might ask them to read a problem and underline the data that are connected.

The Art Club is planning a donut breakfast for its 8 members. The local donut shop recommended that they buy <u>2.5 donuts</u> for <u>each person</u>. How many donuts should they buy? (One person and 2.5 donuts are connected because I need 2.5 donuts for every 1 person.)

One loaf of bread costs $2.79. How much do 6 loaves of bread cost? (One loaf of bread and $2.79 are connected because I need $2.79 for each loaf of bread.)

Once students begin to recognize the data that are connected, we can demonstrate how to create a table with those items. Have pairs or groups of students practice setting up tables from a series of problems. Working with a partner or team will allow students to hear one another's ideas and will help them learn to recognize that when they see a relationship between items in a problem, the creation of a table will be an effective way to organize that data so they can see it more clearly.

Once students are able to recognize a table problem and set up the rows, labeled with each item name, students must use the known data to help them complete the remainder of the table. Consider the previous donut problem. Initially, you may need to talk students through each step to determine how many donuts are needed for 8 people. As students think through the problem, "One person needs 2.5 donuts, so 2 people need 5 donuts," the data can be recorded in the table. Demonstrating by constructing a table on the blackboard or overhead projector as students talk through the missing data will help them visualize the process.

Number of people	1	2	3
Number of donuts	2.5	5	7.5

Students in grades 6 through 8 should be able to create their own tables once they understand how to construct a table to represent data from a problem. It is important to share tables that are both horizontal and vertical. The positioning of the table is not important; it is the organized placement of the data that is essential. Show students that the same data can be represented in different ways as long as the data are organized. Modeling some examples for the class while thinking aloud about which data are connected, how to organize the data on a table, and why a table might be helpful will provide students with opportunities to hear valuable thinking.

Recognizing Patterns and Functions

Although initially students may complete the "Number of donuts" row in the previous problem by adding 2.5 donuts each time they add another person, many will quickly recognize the pattern appearing in the row and simply continue to fill in the numbers as they skip count by 2.5—2.5, 5, 7.5, etc. This recognition of the pattern is an important insight for students and illustrates the power of tables to organize data so that patterns emerge. Sharing observations about patterns will help students recognize the importance of finding a pattern in order to complete tables and, ultimately, solve problems.

Although students may initially see this as a pattern of adding 2.5, multiples of 2.5, or skip counting by 2.5, observation and discussion will lead them to discover another relationship between the numbers in the table. Rather than looking horizontally at the patterns that are created, students might notice that when they look at the vertical columns there is a relationship there, too. Students might observe that the number of donuts is always 2.5 times the number of people. This relationship, which explains the change that is occurring, is called a *function*. As students better understand functions they are able to solve more complex problems. What if the Art Club had 50 members? Knowing the functional relationship of 2.5 donuts for every 1 person allows students to determine that 125 donuts will be needed (2.5 donuts × 50 people). Understanding functions is critical to the study of algebra, and practice with tables will help strengthen this skill. Having students describe the functional relationship in algebraic terms (e.g., $2.5 \times p = d$, where p = number of people and d = number of donuts) helps reinforce important algebra skills.

CLASSROOM-TESTED TIP

Guess My Rule

Use In/Out Tables as a quick warm-up activity to help students explore tables and share their insights about the patterns and functions they see. Put a blank table, on the blackboard, overhead projector, or on chart paper. Begin to fill in a value in the "In" column and then place a value in the "Out" column, challenging students to come up with the rule to explain how the "Out" value was determined. Do a few examples and then ask students to turn and share their ideas with a partner to engage all students in discussion about what they are observing. Pairs might be asked to share what they believe is the rule. Help students reinforce algebraic thinking by asking them to express the rule using the language of algebra. Rather than saying you doubled the number and subtracted 1, ask students to express it as "$2n - 1$". Vary this activity by asking students to work with a partner to develop a rule and then see if the class can guess their rule.

IN	OUT
4	7
6	11
8	15
n	$2n - 1$

Selecting the Correct Answer

A final stumbling block for students in solving problems by making tables comes after the table is created. Many students are quick to recognize the relationship and create the table but have a difficult time choosing the correct answer from the many numbers recorded in the table. This is a critical step, since the creation of the table alone does not solve the problem—it only provides the data from which the problem can be solved. Discussions and demonstrations about how to locate the answer among all of the values in the table are essential, especially for those students who have not previously worked with tables.

Locating the answer from the data in a table begins with locating the "known" data, which then leads students to the "unknown" data. First, ask students to go back to the question: How many donuts do we need for 8 people? Have them locate 8 people in their table and then look for the quantity of donuts that corresponds to that number of people. It will be in the same column, directly above or below the 8 people in a horizontal table, or will be in the same row, next to the 8 people in a vertical table. Teachers might work with a table on an overhead projector or blackboard and place their finger on the number 8 and then move their finger directly up or down on a horizontal table or directly across on a vertical table to find the matching answer, reminding students that rereading the question to find the "known" information is a key to figuring out where to look for the "unknown" information.

Number of people	1	2	3	4	5	6	7	8
Number of donuts	2.5	5	7.5	10	12.5	15	17.5	(20)

Number of people	Number of donuts
1	2.5
2	5
3	7.5
4	10
5	12.5
6	15
7	17.5
8	(20)

Solving More Sophisticated Table Problems

In the middle grades, table problems become increasingly complex. In some cases, the answer to the problem does not appear in the table itself. Consider the following problem:

If you are purchasing cupcakes at $0.69 each, how many cupcakes can you buy for $3.00?

Although $3.00 will not appear in the table, viewing a completed table will help students determine the appropriate answer. When looking at a table like the one that follows, students will see that they will be able to afford 4 cupcakes but not 5.

Number of cupcakes	1	2	3	4	5
Cost	$0.69	$1.38	$2.07	$2.76	$3.45

More sophisticated problems may require tables that have more than two rows or columns, like the following:

André earned $25 from his after-school job. He wants to use this money to treat his friends to a pizza dinner. How many friends can André treat if he buys everyone, including himself, a pizza buffet ($4.49 each) and a drink ($1.79 each)?

There is a relationship between four items, as represented in the following table.

Number of people	1	2	3	4	5
Price for pizza buffets	$4.49	$ 8.98	$13.47	$17.96	$22.45
Price for drinks	$1.79	$ 3.58	$ 5.37	$ 7.16	$ 8.95
Total cost	$6.28	$12.56	$18.84	$25.12	$31.40

The table shows students that André can afford to bring 2 friends plus himself (3 in all) with his $25, or by adding $0.12 to his $25, André can invite 3 friends plus himself (4 in all). André could invite 4 friends plus himself (5 in all) if they ordered pizza and drank only water ($22.45). To reinforce making real-life connections to math problem solving, teachers might ask students to consider the same situation, but have André include a 7% sales tax and 15% tip.

Problems that include data with fractions or decimals integrate problem-solving practice with computational practice. And providing opportunities for students to apply their understanding of tables as they solve problems in geometry will extend their skills in the use of the strategy. Students might be asked to construct rows of connected squares using toothpicks and then to explore the connection between the number of squares in the row and the number of toothpicks used. Their understanding of tables will allow them to organize the data, discover relationships between the data, and solve more complex versions of the problem (i.e., How many toothpicks would be needed to make a row of 50 connected squares?).

Squares	1	2	3	4
Toothpicks	4	7	10	13

By constructing a table, students will gain insight into the relationships between the data and recognize that the initial square requires 4 toothpicks, but each additional square in the row only requires an additional 3 toothpicks. This pattern helps them extend the data even if they do not have enough toothpicks to actually form the rows of squares. And the insight that there is a functional relationship ($3x + 1$, or triple the number of squares and add 1 more to get the number of toothpicks) will allow students to quickly find the number of toothpicks needed to construct a row of 20 squares or 50 squares or 100 squares. The goal is to continue to challenge students with problems that push their thinking and to help them know that they have the foundational skills to tackle increasingly complex tasks. Always ask questions to ensure that students are looking at both patterns and functions and provide them with frequent opportunities to discuss the values they see in the table, especially when using more complicated data.

CLASSROOM-TESTED TIP

Using Recipe Data in Tables

Recipes provide the perfect real data to explore tables. Select a recipe with data that work for the level of your students. Tell students that you are going to continue to increase the recipe so it will feed more people. Have them construct tables to show the data as the quantities are increased. Or to stimulate quick but thoughtful discussions, challenge students by providing them with a table with missing data, as shown in the example that follows. Ask students to decide what is missing and explain how they know what the missing values should be. Ask questions to ensure that students are looking at both patterns and functions in the table.

Peanut Ice Cream Bars

Number of Batches	1	2	3	4
Cups of corn syrup	$\frac{2}{3}$		2	$2\frac{2}{3}$
Cups of peanut butter	$\frac{3}{4}$	$1\frac{1}{2}$		3
Cups of crispy rice cereal	4	8	12	
Gallons of ice cream		1	$1\frac{1}{2}$	2

Using Tables to Connect to Other Math Skills

Students begin using tables to organize data and observe relationships between the data. Insights about their tables and the data in the tables often lead them to insights about other math concepts and alternate ways of finding solutions. After discussing the table that follows, which shows the cost for a school carnival (admission is free, but tickets for games and food are 3 for $5), seventh graders made the following comments as they discussed how they knew that 25 belonged in the blank space in the table:

Tickets	3	6	9	12	15
Cost (in dollars)	5	10	15	20	

"It's 25 because you add 5 more and 20 + 5 = 25." (Notice the recognition of patterns.)

"You could just multiply 5 × 5 because the bottom row is all multiples of five like 1 × 5 and 2 × 5 and 3 × 5 and 4 × 5, so the next one is 5 × 5." (Notice the recognition of multiples.)

"It's like equivalent fractions because $\frac{3}{5}$ is the same as $\frac{6}{10}$ and $\frac{9}{15}$ and $\frac{12}{20}$, so $\frac{15}{25}$ is the same as $\frac{3}{5}$, too." (Notice the understanding of equivalent fractions.)

"The 3 and 5 are two apart, 6 and 10 are 4 apart, 9 and 15 are 6 apart, 12 and 20 are 8 apart, and 15 and 25 are 10 apart." (Notice the recognition of patterns.)

"I don't think you even need all the numbers in between because you could just say $\frac{3}{5}$ and $\frac{15}{25}$ are the same because you multiply the numerator and denominator by 5." (Notice the transition to proportions.)

An insightful student might even notice that the first number + two-thirds of the first number, or five-thirds of the first number, would also equal the second number. $\frac{5}{3} \times 3 = 5; \frac{5}{3} \times 6 = 10; \frac{5}{3} \times 9 = 15$, etc. This type of thinking would reflect recognition of a functional relationship.

Note: Horizontal tables are particularly effective for insights about fractions and proportions because the data are entered in a similar format.

Creating and exploring tables will lead students to insights about other efficient ways to solve problems, including multiplication, proportions, and equivalent fractions. The goal is for students to have a greater repertoire of approaches for solving problems and a better understanding of the math they use to get to solutions. Frequently ask students to explain their insights as they search for patterns and functions and encourage them to discover alternate ways to find answers to problems.

Deciding When to Use a Table

With practice, students will become proficient at creating tables, but the ability to construct a table is only one part of the skills needed. Assisting students in developing the reasoning skill of deciding when this strategy should be used is critical to making it an effective problem-solving tool. After reading a problem that might lend itself to a table, ask students if the problem reminds them of any others they have seen. You might ask them if any of the data are connected, so that when one part changes so does the other. That insight indicates that a table might be an effective way to record and organize the data for further analysis. Asking students to justify their choice of strategies will help you see if they've truly mastered not only the mechanics of the skill but the concept of when it is best used and how it helps them better view and analyze data.

Communicating About the Strategy

Asking students to write about and talk about using tables is a great way to assess their understanding of this strategy. Try prompts like these:

Going to the Movies

Jessalyn earned $40 babysitting and wants to treat her friends to a movie. How many friends can Jessalyn invite if she buys everyone, including herself, a movie ticket, a popcorn, and a drink? How many could she invite if she chose other options (ex. No snacks, sharing snacks, drinking water, etc.)?

Number of people	1	2	3	4	5
Price for movie tickets	$6	$12	$18	$24	$30
Price for drinks	$3.95	$7.90	$11.85	$15.80	$19.75
Price for popcorn	$9.60	$19.20	$28.86	$38.40	$48
Total cost	$19.55	$39.10	$58.65	$78.20	$97.75

What are some of Jessalyn's options?

She could invite all friends and nobody had a snack but all had a ticket and water $30.00 She could take her + a friend and both get a drink and snack. $39.10 She could take three people + they could shared a snack and drink $31.55

Explain how using a table helped you solve this problem.

It told me how much money everything would be so I don't go overboard.

Figure 5–1 *Using a table helped this student determine some of the possible options that were available in the problem.*

▥ Explain how making a table helped you find the answer.

▥ Explain how you know which number in the table is the answer to the problem.

▥ Explain how you know which two (or more) items in the problem should be used to create your table.

▥ Describe the patterns you see on your table.

▨ Explain how you knew when you had enough data in your table to solve the problem.

▨ Why was making a table a good strategy for solving this problem?

A Note About Tables

Not all tables show patterns and functions. Some tables are simply data tables (e.g., a table showing the number of points each player scored in a basketball game or a table to show the cost of tickets for various airline trips). Tables or charts can be used to record a variety of information and may not always show patterns and functions. When we refer to making tables as a problem-solving strategy, however, we are generally referring to those tables that help us explore connected information through patterns and functions as a way of getting to a problem solution. Helping students also see that other data might be recorded on a table, and that data from those tables might be used to solve problems, will build students' understanding of tables as a tool to solve problems. I may need to know how many points each player scored in a basketball game in order to solve a problem asking me to determine the average points scored, but there is not a connection between the number of points scored by each player that allows me to use patterns or functions to complete that table. The data table simply provides me with the necessary information to solve the problem. Teachers might ask students to look at a table and determine whether it has patterns and functions or is simply a data table. Helping students recognize the difference between these types of tables will prevent misunderstandings.

Figure 5–2 *Working with a team allows students to hear one another's ideas and will help them recognize situations when a table will be an effective way to organize data.*

Questions for Discussion

1. How can attention to the Make a Table Strategy help your students learn to organize information? What can you do to ensure that your students recognize that the organization of data is a key for this strategy?

2. How might you simplify this strategy for students who are at a beginning level in their understanding?

3. How might you continue to challenge students who are successfully using tables as a problem-solving tool?

4. In what ways might working with tables reinforce your students' skills and concepts related to basic operations, fractions, and decimals?

CHAPTER 6

Strategy: Make an Organized List

Through group and classroom discussions, students can examine a variety of approaches and learn to evaluate appropriate strategies for a given solution.

—National Council of Teachers of Mathematics,
Curriculum and Evaluation Standards for School Mathematics

While tables, as explored in the previous chapter, provide one way to organize data when there are connections between and among the data, organized lists provide another way. Making an organized list is a valuable strategy when students are faced with problems that require determining all the possible combinations for a given situation. Students might be exploring all the possible double-dip ice cream cone combinations that can be made using vanilla, chocolate, and strawberry ice cream or the number of possible drink/snack combinations that can be made from milk, cola, lemonade, cookies, popcorn, and peanuts. Organizing and recording data in a systematic way helps students keep track of the data and determine all the possibilities.

Organize and Record

The two words describing this strategy—*organized list*—pinpoint the key ideas for the strategy:

1. *List* ideas, or get them out of your head and onto the paper, so you will remember them.

2. Proceed in an *organized* way so you will know what has already been considered and can ensure that no possibilities have been missed.

Recording and organizing information are critical to effective problem solving and yet many students do not intuitively do either when they are faced with a problem. When attempting to figure out all the possible combinations of pizza crusts (thin, regular, deep dish) and single toppings (extra cheese, pepperoni, mushrooms), students often randomly recite possibilities. As students proceed in a random fashion, they become confused and unsure of which combinations have already been given or which combinations have been missed altogether. Teaching students to find a starting point, to begin with one item and then exhaust all possible combinations with that item before moving on to another item, will help them proceed in an organized manner and recognize when they have listed all of the possibilities. Students learn to simplify the task as they are able to keep track of their ideas and double-check their thinking. For example, when listing all possible combinations of single-topping pizzas, a student might begin with the thin crust:

thin crust—extra cheese
thin crust—pepperoni
thin crust—mushrooms

Those are the only toppings, so I'm done with the thin crust. I'll try the regular crust next.

regular crust—extra cheese
regular crust—pepperoni
regular crust—mushrooms

Now I'm done with the regular crust. I'll try the deep dish.

deep dish—extra cheese
deep dish—pepperoni
deep dish—mushrooms

I have no more crusts, so I must be done!

In the middle grades, students transition from recording their ideas on simple lists to the use of more complicated lists or tree diagrams to record the problem information. As students gain confidence with the strategy, continue to challenge them with more difficult problems.

Laying the Foundation for More Sophisticated Skills

Problems that can be solved with an organized list may begin quite simply. In simple combination problems, a goal is to help students understand the importance of finding a starting point and exhausting all possibilities before moving on. Consider the following problem:

> **David wanted to figure out how many different ways his favorite car could be ordered. The car's exterior color could be black, red, blue, or gray. The interior could be cloth or leather. How many different ways could the car be ordered?**

Sixth-grade students attempted to find the sample space, which lists all of the possible car combinations, with the four exterior colors and either a cloth or leather interior. Jennifer said, "I started with the black exterior and gave it a cloth interior and a leather interior. Then I put a red exterior with a cloth interior and a leather interior, then a blue exterior with a cloth or leather interior, and then gray with either cloth or leather. That used all of the exterior colors, so there are 8 ways the car could be ordered." Jennifer recognized that she must have gotten all of the possibilities because she had approached the problem in an organized way and knew that she had found each combination. Jennifer's choice of beginning with a black exterior was a good one, since it is first in the list of exterior colors, but even if she had started with the last exterior color, as long as she moved in an organized manner so she could keep track of what had already been done, she would have been able to find the solution.

Once students have internalized the skill of moving through data in an organized way, helping them explore alternate ways to record their ideas will help them further develop their skills and prepare them for the more sophisticated problems they will face. Students should recognize that using initials or symbols might be more efficient than writing entire words on a list, and so a black exterior becomes *b*, red becomes *r*, blue becomes *bl*, and gray becomes *g*. Tree diagrams are a great way to help students organize their data. The thinking skill of beginning with one item and exhausting possibilities before moving on to another item is central to the concept of a tree diagram. A tree diagram is another way to help students organize the data as they move through each possibility, as shown in this diagram:

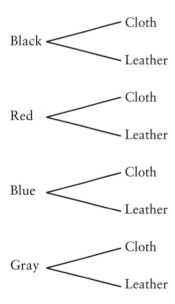

Being able to use organized thinking and to create a tree diagram will support students as they explore the more challenging problem below:

Thomas wanted to figure out how many different ways his favorite car could be ordered. The car's exterior color could be black, red, blue, or gray. The interior could be cloth, leather trim, or all leather. The car could also be ordered with satellite radio or without satellite radio. What are the different ways the car can be ordered?

With the additional data, the problem becomes more confusing. Students who randomly guess possibilities will have a difficult time keeping the data straight without repeating or forgetting possibilities. And recording in a list format requires them to repeatedly write the same words, a lengthy process. Their ability to diagram the possibilities helps to simplify and shorten this otherwise confusing and lengthy task.

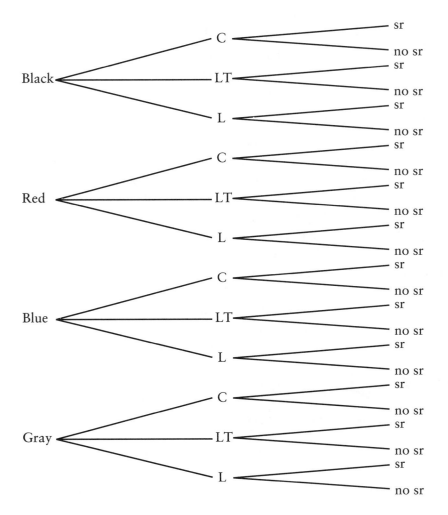

And combination problems can become even more complicated. Students might be asked to find all of the coin combinations they could use to buy a soda for $0.60 if the soda machine will only accept quarters, dimes, and nickels. There are many possible combinations in this problem and many opportunities to become confused. An organized way of recording the data becomes essential. Students can use lessons learned through their experiences with simpler problems to find a starting point, move in a systematic way, and record data in order to keep track of their thinking, as shown in the following table:

Q	D	N
2	1	0
2	0	2
1	3	1
1	2	3
1	1	5
0	6	0
0	5	2
0	4	4
0	3	6
0	2	8
0	1	10
0	0	12

By proceeding in an organized manner, students can determine all of the possibilities. Insights about patterns arise as students notice the patterns in the numbers recorded on their lists. Elizabeth remarked, "Look at the patterns in the nickels column! It always increases by two, but first it's even numbers, then odds, and then evens again!" Jerri said "Every time you subtract one in the dimes column, you increase by 2 in the nickels column." These patterns will only emerge for those students who record information in an organized as opposed to a random way.

What if a problem asks for the possible coin combinations that could be used to buy a bag of chips for $1.29? Finding a way to begin (say, with the coin having the largest value) and exhausting all of the possibilities (and recording each one) before moving to the next coin is of critical importance to simplify these more difficult tasks. As the complexity of problems increases, our students benefit from the foundation skills they have developed through their experiences with simpler problems.

CLASSROOM-TESTED TIP

Looking for Formulas: Combinations

Guide students to a discovery and understanding of the formula for determining the number of combinations. Have students work in groups to solve a combination problem with their organized lists (try the Snack Shop Deals problems on the CD). Change the data for each group (i.e., one group might have a list of 4 cookies, 3 types of fruit, and 2 drinks, while another group will have a list of 3 cookies, 3 types of fruit, and 3 drinks). After each group solves their problem, reorganize the students into new groups of four so they are able to share their data from their original problem with new group members. Have them compile and record their data (number of cookies, number of types of fruit, number of drinks, number of possible combinations) and discuss their observations. Students will observe that 4 cookies, 3 types of fruit, and 2 drinks was ($4 \times 3 \times 2$) 24 possibilities, while 3 cookies, 3 types of fruit, and 3 drinks was ($3 \times 3 \times 3$) 27 possibilities and 5 cookies, 2 types of fruit, and 3 drinks was ($5 \times 2 \times 3$) 30 possibilities. Ask them to come up with a rule (formula) for finding the number of combinations and to try to explain why it will always work. Help students understand that if they have 3 cookies and 2 drinks, each of the 3 cookies could be paired with 2 drinks. This is consistent with the concept of multiplication, where we have 3 groups of 2, or 6 combinations. Once students have used their observations as the basis for possible formulas, getting them involved in discussions to better understand the formulas helps them refine their understanding.

Combinations Versus Permutations

The previous car option problems are examples of combination problems. In combination problems, the order does not matter. A car with a black exterior and a leather interior is the same as a car with a leather interior and a black exterior. They are not two different car option possibilities. The organized list strategy also supports students with permutation problems. In permutation problems, order matters. If Daniel is going to the fair and will ride the roller coaster, scrambler, Ferris wheel, and bumper cars, and we want to figure out all of the different orders in which he might ride the four rides, we find he could ride the roller coaster first, the scrambler second, the Ferris wheel third, and the bumper cars last. Even though it is the same four rides, a different possibility would be to ride the scrambler first, the Ferris wheel second, the bumper cars third, and the roller coaster last. While these problems are a bit different from combination problems, the organized list strategy will support students to simplify the somewhat confusing task. Again, beginning with one ride and exhausting all possibilities with that ride first, before moving to the next ride, would be a good plan to stay on track.

> roller coaster, scrambler, Ferris wheel, bumper cars
> roller coaster, scrambler, bumper cars, Ferris wheel
> roller coaster, Ferris wheel, scrambler, bumper cars
> roller coaster, Ferris wheel, bumper cars, scrambler
> roller coaster, bumper cars, scrambler, Ferris wheel
> roller coaster, bumper cars, Ferris wheel, scrambler
> *There are no other ways to do it with riding the roller coaster first. So let's ride the scrambler first.*

scrambler, roller coaster, Ferris wheel, bumper cars
scrambler, roller coaster, bumper cars, Ferris wheel
scrambler, bumper cars, roller coaster, Ferris wheel
scrambler, bumper cars, Ferris wheel, roller coaster
scrambler, Ferris wheel, roller coaster, bumper cars
scrambler, Ferris wheel, bumper cars, roller coaster
Now, we're done with options for riding the scrambler first, so how about riding the Ferris wheel first?

Ferris wheel, roller coaster, scrambler, bumper cars
Ferris wheel, roller coaster, bumper cars, scrambler
Ferris wheel, scrambler, roller coaster, bumper cars
Ferris wheel, scrambler, bumper cars, roller coaster
Ferris wheel, bumper cars, scrambler, roller coaster
Ferris wheel, bumper cars, roller coaster, scrambler
That's all for riding the Ferris wheel first, so let's list the options for riding the bumper cars first.

bumper cars, roller coaster, scrambler, Ferris wheel
bumper cars, roller coaster, Ferris wheel, scrambler
bumper cars, Ferris wheel, roller coaster, scrambler
bumper cars, Ferris wheel, scrambler, roller coaster
bumper cars, scrambler, Ferris wheel, roller coaster
bumper cars, scrambler, roller coaster, Ferris wheel
There are no more rides, so those must be all of the options!

CLASSROOM-TESTED TIP

Understanding Formulas: Permutations

Ask four students to get in a line to sharpen their pencils. Create the line in front of the class: for example, Katie, then Colleen, then Erica, then Diana. Ask the class how many other ways the students might line up. As class members suggest other ways in which to order the four students, switch their order in the line. After a while, ask students, "Is that all the possible ways? How many ways were there? Are you sure we've tried them all? Are you sure we haven't repeated any?" Ask students to talk with a partner and see if they can figure out a way to be sure that they have identified all the possible orders and haven't repeated any. You might prompt them with questions such as "How many ways can they line up if Katie is first and Colleen is second? What if Katie is first and Erica is second? If Katie is first and Diana is second? Now what if Colleen is first?" Challenge students to find all of the possibilities. Once they have concluded that there are 24 different ways the students could line up, ask them to discuss with their partners how they could have predicted that without listing all of the possibilities. Help them to see that there are 6 different ways to line up with Katie being first. Since each girl could have been first, there would be 6 × 4 or 24 ways to line up. This would also be an excellent opportunity to explore factorials and the formula for determining the number of permutations. Any of the girls could have been first in line, so there were 4 possibilities for the first position. However, when we get to the second position, there were only 3 possibilities since one of them was already in the first position. This means that there were 2 possibilities for third position and only 1 possibility for fourth. Therefore, there were 4 × 3 × 2 × 1 or 24 possibilities. Encourage students to relate this to the organized list or tree diagram that they used for this problem. Connecting their own strategies to the formula $[n \times (n-1) \times (n-2) \times (n-3)]$ will deepen their understanding of why the formula works.

Formulas and Organized Lists

As students work on organized lists, they develop the groundwork for more sophisticated mathematical skills including mathematical formulas that may help them arrive at answers when data become challenging. Consider a problem in which students need to determine the number of shirt/short combinations possible with 3 shirts (blue, red, and green) and 2 shorts (black and brown). It doesn't matter whether the student records a blue shirt with black shorts or black shorts with a blue shirt; regardless of the order in which they are recorded, the combinations are the same. As students work on similar combination problems, they often notice a formula—if there are x of one item and y of another item, then there are xy possibilities. Students will discover that 3 shirts and 2 shorts will yield 3 × 2 or 6 possible combinations. They have discovered the Fundamental Counting Principle, the formula for finding the number of combinations!

In permutation problems, the order is a critical element in determining the number of combinations. Consider a problem in which students are asked to find the number of possible four-digit numbers that could be created by arranging, but not repeating, the digits 1, 2, 3, and 4. The number 1,234 is different from 1,324, which is different from 2,314. Each ordered group is a different possibility. As students work on similar permutation problems, they develop skills in *factorials*. They may discover that four digits can be arranged in 4 × 3 × 2 × 1 ways or 24 ways. Although this formula is often shared with middle grades students, they benefit from discovering the formula on their own as they record, observe, and discuss their findings. Good problem solvers are constantly observant and look for shortcuts (or formulas) based on their observations!

When first using formulas, students may continue to use lists to verify their answers and test to be sure that the formulas will yield the correct results. Mary said, "I think the answer will be 24 because there are 4 exterior car colors, 3 choices for the interior, and 2 choices for radio. Yesterday we had 3 types of pizza crust, 3 types of toppings, and 2 choices for drinks, and we got 18 possibilities, so I think we just do 4 × 3 × 2 to get the answer." Mary's hypothesis was built on observations of previous problems, but she continued to create organized lists to check her thinking until she was convinced that her formula would work. Predicting and testing ideas is an effective way for students to explore, understand, and retain mathematical formulas.

Formulas can provide a shortcut for solving problems, but are not always the best approach. In the problem in Figure 6–1, students are asked to determine how many combinations are possible for 3 types of pants, 3 types of tops, and 2 types of shoes. Students might make an organized list or use a formula to find the number of choices possible. However, if there were 7 types of pants, 9 types of tops, and 6 types of shoes, it would be helpful to know the formula since a list of 378 possibilities would be quite lengthy to construct! The formula allows us to determine the answer even when the data are lengthy and complicated. But a formula is not always the best

Ashley's New Clothes

For her birthday, Ashley got to buy some new clothes. She chose 3 pairs of pants; jeans, khakis, and shorts. She also chose 3 tops; a tank top, t-shirt, and hoodie. Then she selected two pairs of shoes; sandals and sneakers. If Ashley can mix-and-match all of her new purchases, how many outfit combinations (pants, top, shoes) can she make?

Ashley can make _____18_____ outfits.

Show your work.

Pants   tops   shoes
1 2 3   4 5 6   7   8

1,4,7   2,4,7   3,4,7
1,5,7   2,5,7   3,5,7
1,6,7   2,6,7   3,6,7
1,4,8   2,4,8   3,4,8
1,5,8   2,5,8   3,5,8
1,6,8   2,6,8   3,6,8

the #'s under the pants, shorts, and tops are just to represent them.

How did making an organized list help you solve this problem?

First I drew the clothing, then I put the # 1-8 on the bottom of each one then made like diffrent combanitons (using the #'s as like a short cut to not having to draw out the clothes) And then in the end I got 18 diffrent combanotions.

Figure 6–1 *This student used illustrations and numbers to simplify her organized list.*

route to an answer. What if the question had not asked for the number of possibilites, but rather asked the student to list the possible combinations? Now the formula does not lead us to the answer. Or if the problem had listed the prices for each type of pants, tops, and shoes and then asked which pants/top/shoes combinations Ashley could buy if she had $50.00 (or some other designated amount of money), the formula would not allow us to take all of the data into consideration. The new question is not asking how many combinations are possible, but is asking which combinations fit a certain set of criteria. To solve that problem, students need to determine the possible combinations and then do the computations to see which would work for Ashley. Both organized thinking and the use of formulas help us solve problems. Students who have facility with both, and who understand when each one makes sense, are more likely to find solutions to the varied problems they might face.

Communicating About the Strategy

Don't forget to have students write about and talk about their strategy for solving the problem. Try prompts like these:

- Explain why it's important to be organized when making your list.

- How did making a list help you solve this problem?

- Why is it important to record your combinations?

- How are tree diagrams and organized lists alike? How are they different?

- Are you sure there are no other possible combinations? Why?

- Why was making a list a good strategy for solving this problem?

- Is there a way to solve this problem other than making a list? Explain.

In Figures 6–2 and 6–3, students are asked to share tips for solving this type of problem. In order to write their tips, these students had to identify and verbalize key understandings about this problem-solving strategy. In addition to stimulating their thinking and providing practice with communicating that thinking, their written responses allowed their teacher to assess their problem-solving skills, with one student listing all possibilities to find a solution and the other identifying a formula.

Questions for Discussion

1. Why is it important for teachers to think aloud while demonstrating this problem-solving strategy?

2. What are *combinations*? What are *permutations*? How are they alike and different?

The Line-Up

Deuce, Marques, Reggie, and John don't have anything to do next weekend so they decide to go to a movie. How many different ways can they line up to buy the tickets?

D, M, R, J	M, D, R, J	R, J, D, M	J, D, M, R	Deuce = D
D, M, J, R	M, D, J, R	R, J, M, D	J, D, R, M	Marques = M
D, R, M, J	M, J, D, R	R, M, D, J	J, M, D, R	Reggie = R
D, R, J, M	M, J, R, D	R, M, J, D	J, M, R, D	John = J
D, J, R, M	M, R, J, D	R, D, M, J	J, R, D, M	
D, J, M, R	M, R, D, J	R, D, J, M	J, R, M, D	

Deuce · · · · Marques · · · · Reggie · · · · John

24 ways

Share tips for solving this type of problem.

* Abbreviate topics.
* Check to see if you repeated.
* Always start with one thing and find all possible ways, then go to next thing.
* Get organized.
* Move on order.
* Think about shortcuts.
* Write down data.

Figure 6–2 *This student solved the problem by listing all of the possible ways that the boys could line up to buy the tickets.*

3. How might you teach both the organized thinking skill and the formulas? How can you help students understand when each might be helpful?

4. How does using lists help students make complicated problems simpler? Is helping students find a way to make hard problems easier a goal of problem-solving instruction? Why?

The Line-Up

Deuce, Marques, Reggie, and John don't have anything to do next weekend so they decide to go to a movie. How many different ways can they line up to buy the tickets?

Deuce, Marques, Reggie, and John

D, M, J, R
D, M, R, J
D, J, R, M
D, J, M, R
D, R, M, J
D, R, J, M

$4 \times 6 = 24$

Key: Deuce=D
Marques=M John= J
Reggie=R

Share tips for solving this type of problem.

Make an answer key.
Organize your possibilities.
Do possibilities for one person then
multiply by the number of people
for a quick and easy answer.

Figure 6–3 *This student used a shortcut to solve the problem.*

Strategy: Draw a Picture or Diagram

The act of representing encourages children to focus on the essential characteristics of a situation.

—National Council of Teachers of Mathematics,
Curriculum and Evaluation Standards for School Mathematics

The old adage, "A picture is worth a thousand words," can be true in problem solving. Constructing a picture or diagram helps students visualize the problem. In problem solving, we encourage students to get problems out of their heads and into a concrete form. For elementary school students, we begin by acting out problem situations as we add candy to a dish and then move to manipulatives (e.g., cubes or counters) to represent the candy, still allowing students to visualize the situation. As students get older, they may continue to benefit from acting out problems, using real objects, and using manipulatives to represent problem situations, but we mainly support students as they strengthen their skills at creating diagrams as pictorial representations of the problem. After reading a problem, students in the middle grades should be able to use the data to create a diagram that represents the problem situation. Problems that initially appear complex often become easier to solve when students are able to draw or diagram them. Consider the following problem:

> **The eighth grade is planning a Valentine's Day Dance in the school gym. There will be 98 people attending the dance. The school has 3 rectangular tables that each seat 8. They also have round tables that seat 5 and square tables that seat 4. How can they select tables to use so that they use the least number of tables?**

While the data may be difficult to process in our heads, a diagram of the gym will allow us to see the placement of the tables and count how many each table will seat

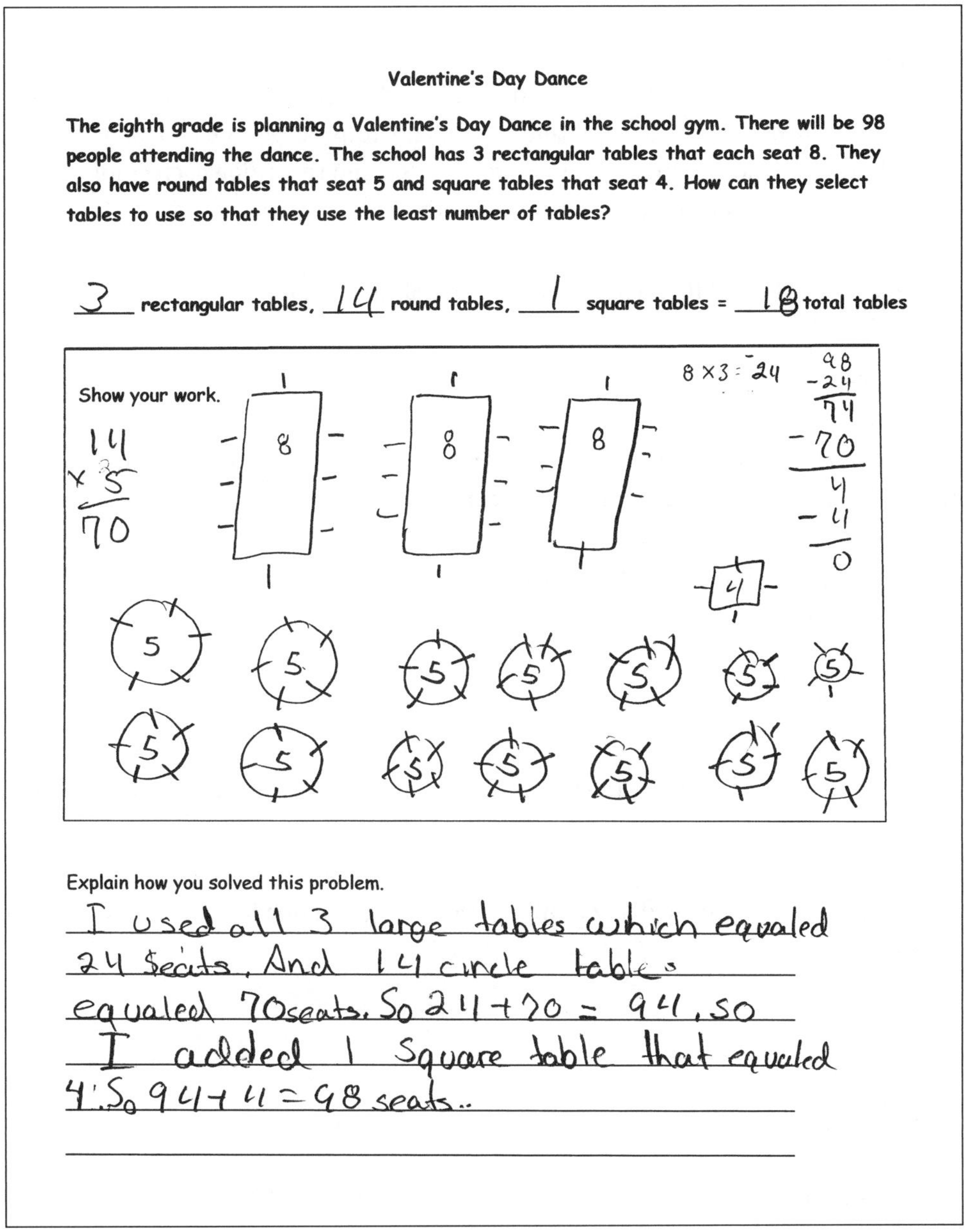

Figure 7–1 *This student's diagram made the problem easier to solve.*

to reveal the least number of tables needed. The problem is immediately simplified by creating a diagram of the data as in the student work in Figure 7–1.

Simplifying Through Diagrams

There were 5 flags flying above the entrance to the amusement park. Each flag was flying at a different level. The red flag was flying higher than the green one. The yellow flag was lower than the green one. The purple flag was higher than the green one but lower than the red one. The blue flag was a little lower than the yellow one. What was the order of flags from highest to lowest?

This type of problem often generates immediate anxiety because of the overload of information and confusing wording; however, if students are able to draw a diagram to represent each piece of information, the problem becomes simple. A diagram serves to clarify the problem situation. It allows students to proceed one clue at a time, so it simplifies the task. By simply moving step by step and recording each color of flag, students can proceed through the problem with ease.

First fact: **The red flag was flying higher than the green one.**

red
green

This fact is represented by the red flag being written above (indicating flying higher than) the green flag in the simple diagram.

Second fact: **The yellow flag was lower than the green one.**

red
green
yellow

If the yellow flag is flying lower than the green flag, that color is recorded below green in the diagram.

Third fact: **The purple flag was higher than the green one but lower than the red one.**

red
purple
green
yellow

If the purple flag is higher than the green flag but lower than the red one, it will need to be recorded between those two colors.

Fourth fact: **The blue flag was a little lower than the yellow one.**

red
purple
green
yellow
blue

The blue flag is lower than the yellow, so it must be the lowest. Blue is recorded at the bottom of the diagram.

Now the diagram is complete, and not only can students clearly see the order of the flags, but there is a sense of accomplishment in solving this initially confusing problem. When asked what was hard about the problem, one sixth grader commented, "There was so much information. I had trouble remembering the order until I wrote it down." She then explained how she made the problem easier to solve by saying, "I didn't understand how to figure this out until I drew a picture. That made it much easier. I didn't have to do it all in my head. I could just see where each flag should be." (*Note:* As students share approaches for solving this problem, a frequent insight is to leave spaces between items as they are recorded. Students report that it allows them to insert information at any place in their diagram. This insight shows the development of their skill with the strategy.)

CLASSROOM-TESTED TIP

Using Manipulatives to Introduce the Strategy

Problems that can be simplified through diagrams often sound quite confusing. Many students experience immediate anxiety and put their pencils down or their heads down, knowing that they cannot solve the complicated problem. If students are not ready to represent a problem using a diagram, the use of manipulatives is a great way to engage them in problem solving and show them that problems often appear more difficult than they may actually be. Begin by posing a problem like the following:

> **Timothy's mother brought home a large chocolate bar for Timothy and his sister to share equally. However, Timothy's sister grabbed the chocolate bar and ate $\frac{1}{6}$ of it. Timothy asked his sister to give him his $\frac{1}{2}$ of the chocolate bar. If she gives Timothy his half and then she eats $\frac{1}{4}$ of what is left, how much of the chocolate bar will his sister have left?**

Provide each pair of students with fraction bars or fraction strips made of paper. Ask them to model the whole chocolate bar and then to show the chocolate bar after Timothy's sister ate $\frac{1}{6}$ of it. Next ask students to show what Timothy's sister's portion of the chocolate bar would look like after she gave him his half. If students remove $\frac{1}{2}$ of $\frac{5}{6}$ rather than $\frac{1}{2}$ of the whole bar, remind them that Timothy and his sister were supposed to share the bar equally, so he should get $\frac{1}{2}$ of the whole bar. Encourage students to talk it through with their partners as they create their chocolate bar models. Look around the room at the fraction bars to see which pairs may need help. Once students have the answer, talk about the level of difficulty of the problem. Was it easier than they thought it would be? What made it easier? If they didn't have the manipulatives, how might they make it easier? The manipulatives allow students to do the problem one clue at a time, to remove portions of the chocolate bar as they are removed in the problem, and to record or remember what has been done. Once students' anxiety is lower, transition them into using paper-and-pencil sketches to do similar problems. Building skills and alleviating anxiety work hand-in-hand to create better problem solvers!

Focusing on More Complex Problems

Initially, problems help students see the power of diagrams to simplify problems.

> **Lauren and her father planted a row of 4 trees in their yard. Now they want to plant some bushes. If they plant 2 bushes at the start of the row of trees, 2 bushes after the last tree, and 3 bushes between each pair of trees, how many bushes will they need to plant?**

Students can simply draw the 4 trees, represent the appropriate number of bushes at each location, and count or add to find the solution. As students master representing data with diagrams, however, we challenge them with additional criteria.

There is added complexity in this soccer tournament problem:

> **There were 6 teams in the soccer tournament. The Jaguars finished ahead of the Tigers. The Lions finished behind the Tigers. The Bulldogs finished between the Jaguars and the Tigers. The Bears finished ahead of the Jaguars. The Mustangs finished behind the Lions. What was the order of the teams from first to last?**

Students' confusion about order becomes apparent in this type of problem as they begin to represent the information and lose track of which team finished "first" and which finished "last." As students share their ways of recording the data, others will gain tips like recording "first" and "last" on their papers.

| First | Bears Jaguars Bulldogs Tigers Lions Mustangs | Last |

Discussing the parts of a problem that make it more challenging is an important component of the problem-solving experience.

Students will continue to face problem situations of increasing complexity, such as the following problem:

> **I have 1 large bag. Inside the large bag are 2 medium bags. Inside each medium bag are 3 small bags. Inside each small bag are 3 tiny bags. Inside each tiny bag are a quarter and a dime. How much money is in my bag? I plan to use the money in my bag to buy candy. Each piece of candy costs $0.20. How many pieces of candy can I buy?**

This multi-step problem could be simplified through a diagram to allow students to visualize the number of bags (and number of coins). Students, however, will also need to use their understanding of money, as well as their computation skills, to find the solution. As problems get more complex, they push students to apply a variety of math skills.

> **Abby is helping her father fence in a part of the yard for a garden. The area they are fencing in is 15 feet wide and 10 feet long. They need to put a post in the ground every $2\frac{1}{2}$ feet. How many posts will they need?**

To find a solution, students use their understanding of measurement and their computation skills, but are often jump-started by drawing the garden. The drawing allows them to visualize the problem situation, but it is only the first step to finding the answer. As students experience success with simple problems, challenge them with problems that require them to merge their understanding of the strategy with other math skills (e.g., measurement, operations, fractions, decimals).

Differentiating Instruction Through Problem Solving

Often students within the same classroom are at a variety of levels in their understanding and use of problem-solving strategies. Differentiating problems for varied groups within the classroom allows teachers to explore a similar strategy while supporting students by providing appropriate levels of challenge. A seventh-grade teacher posed this problem to her class:

> **Emma helped her father wallpaper her bedroom. They wallpapered $\frac{2}{3}$ of the room before taking a break. After the break, they wallpapered $\frac{1}{2}$ of what was left. How much of the room still needs wallpaper?**

While some students were able to determine the answer using their computational skills, many drew a rectangle or similar shape to represent the entire room, divided it into 3 equal parts, and shaded in 2 of the 3 to show the part of the room that was wallpapered before the break. Then they divided the remaining $\frac{1}{3}$ into 2 equal parts and shaded one of them. This allowed them to see that $\frac{1}{6}$ of the room still needed wallpaper. But, for one group in the class, the teacher posed a variation of the problem that was a bit more complex:

> **Emma helped her dad wallpaper her bedroom. They wallpapered $\frac{2}{3}$ of the room before taking a break. After the break, they realized that $\frac{1}{8}$ of the wallpaper had fallen off. How much of the room still needs wallpaper?**

By adding additional data and the condition that $\frac{1}{8}$ of the wallpaper had fallen off, this problem challenged students beyond the original version of the problem. Adding layers of complexity to problems for specific students will keep them engaged and continue to push their thinking skills.

Working in groups has many benefits in problem-solving instruction. It allows students to share ideas and hear each other's thinking. But students often work at different speeds, with some groups finishing while others are still actively engaged with the task. Teachers might consider posing a problem to all groups and asking groups to raise their hands as they finish the task. The teacher can then move to that group and ask them to explain or justify their answer in order to check their understanding. If students are ready to move on, the teacher might have a second-tier task ready to keep them involved in the activity. The bag and coins problem described previously might be adapted to fit this instructional model.

Task 1: **I have 1 large bag. Inside the large bag are 2 medium bags. Inside each medium bag are 3 small bags. Inside each small bag are 3 tiny bags. Inside each tiny bag are a quarter and a dime. How much money is in my bag?**

As groups complete the task, they raise their hands and the teacher joins their group. Group members justify their answers to the teacher, and then a second part of the task is assigned.

Task 2: **I plan to use the money in my bag to buy candy. Each piece of candy costs $0.20. How many pieces of candy can I buy?**

For the first part of the problem, students might draw a diagram to find the solution, but the second part requires using the answer to the first part along with an understanding of money and computational ability to find the amount of candy that can be bought. "What if" questions work well to extend thinking for groups who finish quickly. *What if* there were 2 large bags? *What if* there were 2 quarters and two dimes in each tiny bag? *What if* the candy cost $0.25 per piece?

A diagram can provide students with a starting point for solving a problem. Analyzing their own diagram can then help them transition into more abstract methods. Mrs. Kelly posed the following problem to her students:

Coach Gibbs organized a luncheon to celebrate the baseball team's first-place finish. The restaurant had square tables with only one person being able to sit on each side of the table. Coach Gibbs asked the restaurant manager to push tables together to make one long row of 9 tables and said that every seat would be filled. How many people were seated at the luncheon?

Some students immediately created equations to solve the problem, but Clint and Sean drew a diagram of the row of tables, marking an x where each person would sit. Mrs. Kelly asked them to explain how they solved the problem, and Clint explained that they added the 9 people on one side to the 9 on the other side of the row and then added the two people who would sit on the ends of the long row and got 20 people. Another group shared their equation: $2(9) + 2 = 20$. Sean looked at his diagram and added, "That's what we did! It's just 2×9 because there are 2 rows with 9 in each row and then we added the 2 on the end!" Sean had made the connection between his diagram and the other group's equation.

CLASSROOM-TESTED TIP

The Value of Modeling and Discussions

At times it becomes obvious that simplifying problems with diagrams may not be intuitive for all students. We notice that students become frustrated when we pose problems that appear confusing. It may be helpful to do some modeling for students by using think-alouds to share our thinking, asking questions, and supporting them as we explore a problem together.

> **Emma helped her dad wallpaper her bedroom. They wallpapered $\frac{2}{3}$ of the room before taking a break. After the break, they realized that $\frac{1}{8}$ of the wallpaper had fallen off. How much of the room still needs wallpaper?**

While some students may immediately see how drawing a diagram is a way to simplify this problem, others will shut down as they are initially confused by the data. Support students by exploring the problem together. Ask them if seeing a diagram of the problem might help them find the answer. Have them draw a diagram to represent the room, and then ask them to show how much of the room was wallpapered before the break. They will most likely divide their "room" into thirds and shade or mark out two of the sections. Ask students to draw another diagram of the room to reflect how it looked after Emma and her father returned from their break. They will have to convert the $\frac{2}{3}$ (the part of the room that was wallpapered) into eighths and circle one of these sections to represent the wallpaper that fell off and must be redone. Help students to understand that this section represents $\frac{1}{8}$ of the area that was wallpapered, but $\frac{1}{12}$ of the whole room. Dividing the entire "room" into twelfths will help them see that Emma still needs to wallpaper the remining $\frac{4}{12}$ of the room plus the $\frac{1}{12}$ that fell off, or $\frac{5}{12}$ of the entire room. Ask students to talk about what was easy or hard about the problem and how the diagram helped them solve it.

Communicating About the Strategy

Don't forget to have students write and talk about their strategies. Impromptu teacher questioning and informal discussions help students solidify their understandings and provide opportunities for them to reflect on their approaches (see Figure 7–2). In addition, reviewing students' writing and listening to their discussions are great ways for teachers to get a glimpse of students' thinking. Try prompts like these:

- Why was drawing a diagram a good strategy for solving this problem?

- Does a diagram need to be detailed to help you solve a problem? Explain.

- Explain how your diagram helped you solve this problem.

- Can a picture or diagram help you find errors in your thinking? Explain.

- How did a diagram help you better understand this problem?

Figure 7–2 *Ongoing teacher support helps students clarify their thinking and identify appropriate problem-solving strategies.*

Questions for Discussion

1. How can the use of pictures and diagrams simplify difficult tasks?

2. Diagrams help students visualize problems. How is the use of manipulatives similar to using pictures and diagrams? How is it different? How is acting out a problem situation similar to using pictures and diagrams? How is it different?

3. How might teachers help students see a variety of ways to diagram a problem?

4. How might teachers challenge different levels of students in the same classroom?

5. How might diagramming a problem help students transition to more abstract ways to solve problems?

Strategy: Guess, Check, and Revise

When problem solving becomes an integral part of classroom instruction and children experience success in solving problems, they gain confidence in doing mathematics and develop persevering and inquiring minds.

—National Council of Teachers of Mathematics,
Curriculum and Evaluation Standards for School Mathematics

The Guess, Check, and Revise strategy is exactly what it sounds like—if you're not sure where to begin, take a guess! The guess, however, should be reasonable and is only the beginning of the process. After plugging the guess into the problem situation, a student will need to adjust the guess until the correct answer is found.

Beginning with a Guess

Often students are faced with a problem and they don't know how to begin. While a guess may be a good way to begin tackling the problem, the guess should be a reasonable one. Students should be able to use their number sense and estimation skills to get "in the ballpark." Discuss initial guesses with students. Together, look for clues in the problem that will help them make educated guesses and in so doing, lessen the number of revisions they will have to make. If a problem asks for three consecutive numbers that have a sum of 144, students should not be starting with a guess of 100. It would not be reasonable to think that 100, 101, and 102 would add up to 144. If you notice unreasonable student guesses, practice just the first step of this problem-solving strategy. Pose problems to your students and ask them to estimate (guess) the answer. Have students discuss the reasonableness of their guesses with a partner or team. Ask them to share their ideas on how they came up with their guesses. Logical reasoning and number sense play an important role in this strategy.

Revising the Guess

Revision is a critical step in this strategy. It is unlikely that students will guess the correct answer on the first try, so they must then plug their guesses into the problem and adjust the initial guess until they've found the correct answer. Students will need to recognize when their guess is too large or too small and will need to be able to make adjustments until the answer is found. Consider this problem:

> **Jenny and Brad were playing cards. When the game ended, Brad had scored 120 points less than Jenny. Together they had 430 points. How many points did each person score?**

Josh was confused and did not know where to begin, so he started with a guess.

> *"Jenny had 300 points. So Brad had 180 points because he had 120 points less than Jenny."*

That would be a total of 480 points, which is too much. The guess was a reasonable one, but did not prove to be the correct answer. Josh needed to adjust his guess so that the sum of their money was less. He decided to try this:

> *"Jenny had 260 points and Brad had 140 points so they had 400 points together. That's not enough."*

Josh realized he needed to increase the amounts.

> *"280 + 160 = 440 points. That's a little too many!"*
> *"275 + 155 = 430 points. That's it!"*

Josh did several revisions before he arrived at the correct answer, but the revisions were thoughtful ones. He was using the data he observed to make each new adjustment. When evaluating student work, look for evidence that each revision leads students closer to the answer.

Thinking aloud is especially important when demonstrating this strategy. Both in selecting a first guess and in revising guesses throughout the process, it is important that students understand the thinking involved in each step. Students need to hear your thought processes as you adjust and readjust your answers. Students need to know it's okay not to get the answer on the first guess. After modeling a few problems for the class, you might want to ask students to work with a partner to hear each other's thinking during the revision stage.

As problems become more confusing, students may need encouragement to come up with their initial guess and may benefit from teachers setting up the problem with the whole class. Consider this problem:

Caroline's age this year is a multiple of 5. Next year, Caroline's age will be a multiple of 4. How old is Caroline now?

The problem initially feels complex, and students may not know where to begin. Teachers who acknowledge the confusing feel to a problem will help to relieve students' initial anxiety.

MS. HILL: This problem looks really confusing. Let's talk about it together for a minute. What can we do to make it simpler? Talk to your partner about a way to get started.

(Students talk in pairs about ways to begin the problem.)

MS. HILL: What could we try?

STUDENT: We could just guess an age for Caroline.

STUDENT: We could try that she's 8 this year.

STUDENT: No, she can't be 8; it's not a multiple of 5.

MS. HILL: What do you mean?

STUDENT: The problem says her age is a multiple of 5 this year, so we have to start with a multiple of 5.

MS. HILL: So what might be a good guess? Turn to your partners and tell them a possible age for Caroline.

(She asks students to share some of their possibilities, which include 10, 25, 5, and 15.)

STUDENT: We could say Caroline is 5, since that's the first multiple of 5. Next year she'll be six. But it won't work.

MS. HILL: Why not?

STUDENT: Because next year her age has to be a multiple of 4, and 6 isn't a multiple of 4.

MS. HILL: So this is getting confusing. Turn to your partner and see if you can come up with a way to make this less confusing.

(Students share their ideas, including one pair's suggestion that they could "make a list of all of the multiples of 5 and then add one to each one. Then we could find the one that is a multiple of 4.")

MS. HILL: Think about the different ideas that have been shared and work with your partners to solve this problem.

Whole-class discussions at the start of the problem give students a chance to process the task and think through a method of approaching the task. Next, they can use their knowledge of Guess, Check, and Revise thinking, their understanding of multiples, and their ability to organize and record data to gather the data they will need to find a solution (or more than one solution). Class discussions get students thinking about the task and focus them on some potential challenges and possible approaches.

C L A S S R O O M - T E S T E D   T I P

Modeling Guess, Check, and Revise Thinking

Cut out ads for six different articles of clothing from a department store adver-tisement, for example, jeans: $23.95; sweatshirt: $19.99; jacket: $49.99, sweater: $21.98; shorts: $14.99; and tee shirt: $9.99. Tell the students that you bought two of the items and the total cost was $34.98 (or an amount that makes sense with your data). They will need to figure out which two items you bought. Have a student guess two items. Together, figure out the cost of those items. Ask the students to tell you if these two items cost too much, too little, or just the right amount. If the guess was not correct, tell the students that they will need to try again. Ask for another guess, but this time ask them to use what they now know to get closer to the answer. After the revised guess ask students, "Is the guess too high, too low, or just right?" Students may be asked to respond with thumbs up (too high), thumbs down (too low), or a flat hand parallel to the ground (just right).

Ask students if there are any items that could not possibly be the items that you bought at the store and to justify why (i.e., the jacket, because it costs more than the total cost). Continue until you've found an answer. Try a few more, with students working in pairs or groups to allow them to discuss their guesses and revisions.

Using Guess, Check, and Revise with Equations

A student might look at the following equation and not know where to begin. This is when students often put their heads down or choose not to proceed because they don't know how to get started. The Guess, Check, and Revise strategy will provide them with both a starting point and a method to figure out the answer.

$$4 \times \underline{\hspace{1cm}} - 7 = 27$$

Encourage them to try a number in the blank—for example, 4.

$4 \times 4 - 7 = 27$??? Actually, $4 \times 4 - 7 = 9$. "This answer is too small, so let's try a larger number. How about 8?"

$4 \times 8 - 7 = 25$ "Closer, but still too small. How about 9?"

$4 \times 9 - 7 = 29$ "Now it's too big. Would 8.5 work?"
$4 \times 8.5 - 7 = 27$ "It worked! 8.5 is the correct answer."

Without knowing how to begin, the student was able to find the correct answer by using the Guess, Check, and Revise method. Although students in grades 6 through 8 are learning techniques for solving problems with equations (e.g., using inverse operations), our goal is to arm students with varied ways to find solutions and enhance their repertoire of strategies so they have options as they attempt the varied problems they face. Ultimately, our goal is for students to solve problems in the most efficient way possible, but the ability to guess, check, and revise to find an answer will offer a starting point for students who might otherwise be overwhelmed with the task.

Understanding the Role of Positive Attitudes

This strategy depends on the development of positive problem-solving attitudes, as discussed in the Introduction. Students must be risk takers and be willing to jump in, even when they are unsure how to begin. Students are sometimes hesitant to guess an answer. Assure them that it is a fine way to begin a problem—as long as they check their guess and adjust it as needed. Students must also be patient and persistent as they check and revise each guess. Each guess should bring them closer to the correct answer.

Using Combined Strategies

Although we are focusing on specific problem-solving strategies in this book in order to develop our understanding of each strategy, many problems require students to use the thinking skills from several strategies. Consider the following problem:

> **Paige is selling bracelets for $5.75, $6.50, and $7.50. Tiffany wants to buy some bracelets from Paige. How might Tiffany spend no more than $20 on bracelets?**

Using Guess, Check, and Revise thinking will lead students to reasonable possibilities, but students might also want to employ their skill of organized, systematic thinking and begin with one of each type of bracelet, try other combinations that make sense, and then move in a systematic way through the other possible combinations of prices in the problem. While they are using organized thinking, they may only be trying those combinations that have the potential to solve the problem—their guess-and-check thinking may have already alerted them to combinations that could not possibly work as the answer (i.e., When questioned by the teacher, the student in Figure 8–1 explained there was no reason to try three $7.50 bracelets, because they would cost more than $20!). Combining their knowledge of guess-and-check thinking, their understanding of organized lists, and their knowledge of basic operations will support them in finding the solutions.

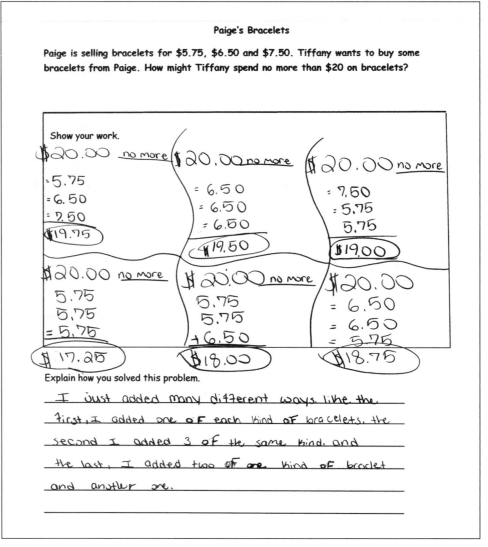

Figure 8–1 *This student found six combinations of bracelets that Tiffany could buy for no more than $20.*

C L A S S R O O M - · T E S T E D   T I P

Cooperative Problem-Solving Cards

In order to stimulate group discussions about problem solving, consider dividing the problem data onto separate index cards and providing each group member with a card that states part of the problem data. Ask students to work together to combine their information and find a solution. For example, in a group of four students, each student might receive one of the following data cards:

Card #1   Some friends are going to the movie theater. The cost for each adult's ticket is $7.75.

Card #2   The cost for each child's ticket is $5.75.

Card #3   The total cost for everyone was $59.75.

Card #4   If there were 9 people going to the movie theater, how many of them were adults and how many were children?

Group members will need to share their information, consider everyone's data, and discuss their approach to solving the problem. A guess-and-check approach might lead them to the solution of 4 adults and 5 children, and the group discussions will allow members to share their confusions and successes. Refer to Cooperative Problem-Solving Cards on the CD for some examples.

Building the Foundation for More Advanced Skills

Although the Guess, Check, and Revise method is used more frequently in primary and intermediate grades because students in the middle grades transition to using algebraic equations to find answers to similar problems, this strategy still provides a means to a solution for those middle grades students who are struggling. It also helps strengthen students' number sense and their ability to assess the reasonableness of answers as they revise and adjust their guesses. Classroom discussions in which students share their solution strategies are an important way to encourage middle grades students to understand that there are more efficient ways to solve problems (e.g., algebraic equations). We want them to view Guess, Check, and Revise as a possible, but less frequently relied on, means of solving problems. Consider the following problem, for example:

Ryan's grandparents gave him a gift of $1000. Ryan deposited the money into two accounts, one that pays 6% interest and one that pays 5%. After a year, Ryan has earned $56 in interest. How much did he deposit in each account?

In algebra, you write an equation: $0.06x + 0.05(1000 - x) = 56$. This equation represents an understanding that the solution can be found by adding 6% of a number of dollars (x) and 5% of the remaining dollars ($1000 - x$). In Guess, Check, and Revise, you try a number of dollars invested at 6%, such as $500. That would mean that $500 was also invested at 5% ($1000 – $500). If we add 6% of $500 ($30) plus 5% of $500 ($25), we get $55. That's too low. Time to revise! Try $600 at 6% ($36) and $400 at 5% ($20). The sum would be $56. The Guess, Check, and Revise strategy is another way to solve the same problem. Through sharing problem-solving approaches in the classroom, we discover opportunities to transition students to alternate ways of representing problems. As students share their ideas, we can begin to discuss algebraic ways to find solutions, transitioning students to new approaches.

Communicating About the Strategy

In order to continue to develop students' understanding, don't forget to have students write about and talk about the strategy. Try prompts like these:

- How did you come up with your first guess?

- Explain why revising is so important.

- How did Guess, Check, and Revise help you solve this problem?

- Why did you choose this strategy to help you solve this problem?

- Why is it important to be persistent when solving problems?

Questions for Discussion

1. How does students' number sense affect their ability to effectively use the Guess, Check, and Revise strategy?

2. Can group and partner activities assist the development of the thinking processes needed to effectively use problem-solving strategies? How?

Figure 8–2 *Writing and reflecting about the use of a problem-solving strategy will help develop students' understanding.*

3. How might teachers emphasize the importance of reasonable guesses and reasonable revisions when working on Guess, Check, and Revise thinking?

4. How does the guess-and-check process in math compare with the trial-and-error process in science? Are there other connections between math problem solving and the scientific process?

Strategy: Use Logical Reasoning

Reasoning is fundamental to the knowing and doing of mathematics.

—National Council of Teachers of Mathematics,
Principles and Standards for School Mathematics

Logical reasoning is a critical problem-solving skill. Many of the other strategies we have discussed depend on logical reasoning. Students may need to use logical reasoning as they create pictures or diagrams to represent confusing problem situations or as they employ Guess, Check, and Revise thinking to determine solutions to complex problems. And middle grades students will begin to see the value of strong logical reasoning skills as they delve more deeply into geometry proofs. In many cases, it is hard to separate logical reasoning from other strategies. Some problems, however, utilize logical reasoning as the primary problem-solving strategy. Whether it is the primary strategy or is combined with other problem-solving strategies, logical reasoning is a critical factor in students' problem-solving success.

Logical reasoning is an organized approach to solving problems in which we use good judgment to draw reasonable conclusions. Logic problems often have lots of data that appear confusing, and students are then challenged to make sense of the data and draw conclusions from it. The data do not always directly state ideas but may require students to make an inference (i.e., *John does not use a bat to play his favorite sport. So, John's favorite sport is not baseball, since that sport uses a bat.*). In this strategy, students need to practice analyzing clues or bits of information presented in the problem and then use that information to help solve the problem.

Techniques like process of elimination help students narrow down the possible solutions so they can arrive at a logical answer. Graphic organizers like matrices and Venn diagrams also help students organize data so they are able to clearly see the data

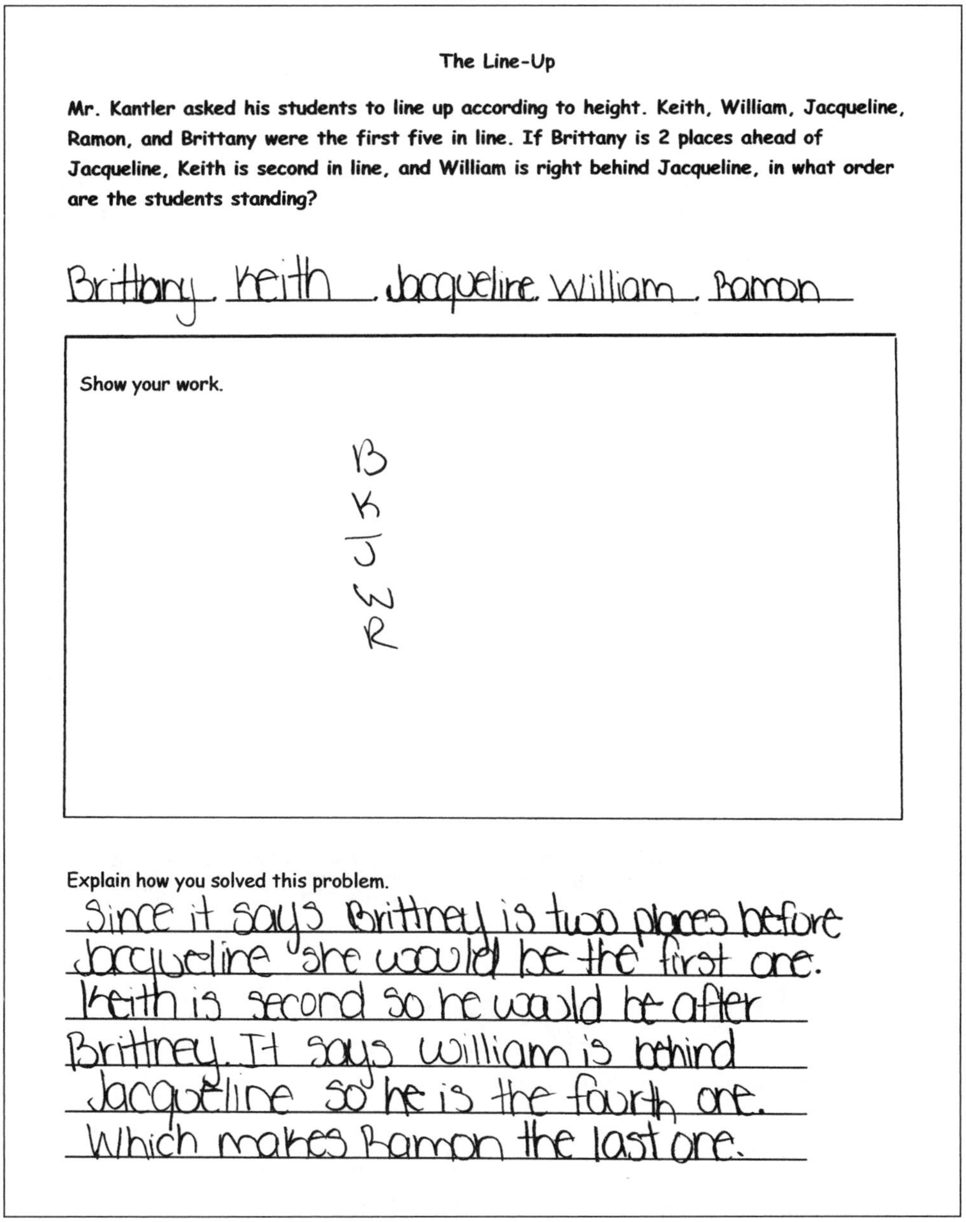

The Line-Up

Mr. Kantler asked his students to line up according to height. Keith, William, Jacqueline, Ramon, and Brittany were the first five in line. If Brittany is 2 places ahead of Jacqueline, Keith is second in line, and William is right behind Jacqueline, in what order are the students standing?

Brittany, Keith, Jacqueline, William, Ramon

Show your work.

B
K
J
W
R

Explain how you solved this problem.

Since it says Brittney is two places before Jacqueline she would be the first one. Keith is second so he would be after Brittney. It says William is behind Jacqueline so he is the fourth one. Which makes Ramon the last one.

Figure 9–1 *This student uses a diagram to help him organize the confusing problem data and draw appropriate conclusions.*

and draw appropriate conclusions. Providing students with opportunities to experience varied logic problems and to discuss their conclusions helps them strengthen their logical reasoning skills.

The Role of Inference

When students are asked to infer, they are being asked to use clues to figure out what is happening in a problem. Often a problem does not come right out and state the necessary data, but rather challenges students to figure out the data by "reading between the lines." Consider the following problem, which requires students to make an inference:

> **Lindsay has a four-scoop ice cream cone. She has a scoop of chocolate, vanilla, banana, and strawberry ice cream. The chocolate ice cream is the last flavor she will eat. The vanilla scoop is not touching the chocolate or the banana. What is the order of the ice cream flavors?**

Information from this problem must be gathered based on students' understanding of the situation and their ability to draw conclusions. If chocolate is the last flavor Lindsay will eat, then it must be scoop #1, the scoop closest to the cone. If the vanilla scoop does not touch the chocolate, then it must be either scoop #3 or #4. Since vanilla also doesn't touch banana, vanilla must be on top. The order from top to bottom must be vanilla, strawberry, banana, then chocolate.

Providing opportunities for students to share what is stated and what is implied will help those who are confused by the problem. Class discussions, think-alouds in which teachers model their skills at making inferences, and partner activities in which students can work together to discuss solutions are helpful instructional techniques. Making inferences is a critical foundation skill for effective logical reasoning.

CLASSROOM-TESTED TIP

If, Then Statements

Completing If, Then statements is a great way to prepare students for more complex geometry where logic plays a role in proofs. Have students complete If, Then statements like the following:

> If a triangle is isoscleles, then . . . (it has at least 2 congruent sides)
> If an angle is right, then . . . (it measures 90 degrees).
> If a fraction is improper, then . . . (its value is greater than 1)

As students share their statements, they may discover that some statements can be completed in more than one way. This discovery can lead to a discussion that is rich with logical reasoning.

Using a Logic Matrix

A matrix is a grid on which students record data. It is a tool for helping students organize information and keep track of their ideas as they work through the process of piecing clues together. Consider the following problem:

Kelly, Jamie, Eric, and Paul all brought their lunches to school. They decided to swap desserts, so each ate one of the other's desserts. Kelly didn't like Eric's dessert, so she chose a different one. Jamie ate Paul's. Whose dessert did Paul eat?

The information is confusing and somewhat jumbled together. In order to find a solution, students have to first find a way to clarify the data so they can look at it clearly to draw conclusions. Creating a grid or matrix like the one in Figure 9–2 allows them to organize the information. Students can begin the matrix by writing in the four names (Kelly, Jamie, Eric, and Paul) and the four possible desserts. Then the clues are read, evaluated, and the conclusions recorded. The matrix supports students as they move toward a solution by allowing them to consider one clue at a time and remember their conclusions since they have been recorded on the matrix.

Each ate one of the other's desserts. *(This means that none of them ate their own dessert. I can put an x in each person's row on the grid under their own dessert.)* Notice the inference!

Kelly didn't like Eric's dessert, so she chose a different one. *(I can put an x in Kelly's row under Eric's dessert.)*

Jamie ate Paul's. *(I can put a yes or check mark in Jamie's row under Paul's dessert. That also means I can put an x in Jamie's row under Eric's and Kelly's desserts since Jamie only had one dessert.)* Eliminating wrong answers will help students narrow down the possibilities.

So, Paul must have eaten Eric's dessert, since no one else did!

By eliminating the other possibilities for Paul, since we know he ate Eric's dessert, we are able to see that Eric ate Kelly's dessert (the only possibility left for Eric). And eliminating the other possibilities for Eric allows us to see that Kelly ate Jamie's dessert.

Each clue brings students closer to a solution. Making inferences helps students make sense of each clue, and the matrix helps them keep track of the clues.

When showing students how to use a matrix, remind them to read and think about each clue and to revisit clues a second time if the problem remains unsolved after they have gone over each clue one time. Often, a clue has more meaning after another clue has been considered. Remind students that when they find an answer, they should eliminate the other boxes in the same row and column. There can only be one *yes* in each row and column. That is an important understanding, as a matrix is used

	Kelly's Dessert	Jamie's Dessert	Eric's Dessert	Paul's Dessert
Kelly	X	yes	X	X
Jamie	X	X	X	yes
Eric	yes	X	X	X
Paul	X	X	yes	X

Figure 9–2 *Information is organized on a matrix.*

when students are looking for a one-to-one match (e.g., which students ate which dessert), so there will only be one student matched with each dessert.

Continue to challenge students with more complex matrix problems. Students might be asked to solve problems with a double or triple matrix in which they must determine the sport played by each of five students, the color of each of their jerseys, and the number that appears on each player's jersey. And as students become proficient with using matrices, provide them with logic problems that do not have the matrix printed on the page, challenging them to recognize when a matrix is a reasonable tool for organizing clues and finding problem solutions. Discussing familiar problems (ones solved in the past) and the methods used to solve those problems often leads students to recognize the appropriateness of using a matrix as a possible tool. Prompting students to create their own matrix to fit the problem criteria (e.g., 4 rows for 4 people, 4 columns for 4 desserts) will refine their skills with this strategy!

Using a List to Organize Clues

A matrix is not the only way to visualize a logic problem. Students can create lists on which they cross off items that are eliminated as possible answers. Figuring out what is not the answer can be an important step toward reaching the actual answer. Consider the following problem:

> **The Hillview Sharks played a football game against the Fairway Tigers. One team's score was a multiple of 7 and less than 26. The other team's score was greater than 7, less than 38, and a multiple of 6. The sum of the digits of this score was 6. The greatest common factor of the two scores was 2. The Tigers won the game. What was the final score?**

Students can keep track of their progress toward a solution by making a list of numbers and then crossing off the unnecessary numbers as they analyze each clue.

Score #1 is a multiple of 7 and less than 26.
(*These are all possibilities.*)

7   14   21

Score #2 is greater than 7, less than 38, and a multiple of 6.
(*These are the possibilities.*)

12   18   24   30   36

The sum of the digits of Score #2 was 6. (*2 + 4 = 6. Score #2 must be 24! I can cross off all but 24.*)

The greatest common factor of the two scores was 2. (*That means that both scores are even. Score #1 must be 14! I can cross off all but 14.*)

The Tigers won the game. (*Final Score: Tigers 24, Sharks 14*)

Football Scores

The Hillview Sharks played a football game against the Fairway Tigers. One team's score was a multiple of 7 and was less than 26. The other team's score was a multiple of 6, was greater than 7, and was less than 38. The sum of the digits of this score was 6. The greatest common factor of the two scores was 2. The Tigers won the game. What was the final score?

Tigers ___24___   Sharks ___14___

Show your work. —One team score was a multiple of 7 $ less than 26.   7·1=7, | 7·2=14 |, 7·3=21

—Other team was a multiple of 6 was greater than 7 $ less than 38.
      6·2=12, 6·3= 18, | 6·4=24 | 6·5=30, 6·6=36

—The sum of the digits for this score was 6.
      Has to be 24 because no other digits add up to equal 6.

—The greatest common factor of the two scores was 2.
   - 24 can go into 2   - 7 can't go into 2
   - 21 can't go into 2   - 14 can go into 2

—Tigers won. So the Tigers scored 24 $ Sharks scored 14

Explain how you solved this problem.

What I did is pretty simple, all I did was right down the important information and come up with possible solutions for each of the information I got. Then when It came down to The Sum of the digits for the second score was 6 I knew it was 24 because no other multiple of 6 that is more then 7 but less then 38 equals 6. After that I got 14 because the GCF is 2 and 7 nor 21 can go into 2 evenly. Finally they said the Tigers won so the highest score went to the Tigers $ the lowest went to the Sharks.

Figure 9–3 *This student used logical reasoning to go through the problem step by step. Although she says, "24 can go into 2" instead of saying, "2 can go evenly into 24," it is clear that she understands the clue about 2 being the greatest common factor.*

While some students may be able to do multiple steps in their heads without recording the data, many benefit from recording and eliminating data as they read and analyze the clues. And again, the process of recording the data ("getting it out of their heads") can simplify an otherwise challenging problem. Hundred charts (see Hundred Charts on the CD) are another tool to allow students to "see" numbers when working with logic number problems. Students might use the hundred charts to record their ideas by crossing off or circling numbers to match the clues.

To stimulate discussion about their thinking, consider having students work in groups of four to solve logic number problems. Give each student in the group a card with a different clue to the mystery number (see the logic examples in the Cooperative Problem-Solving Cards on the CD). Have students share their clues and work together to determine the mystery number. Consider assigning roles to each student (leader, recorder, checker, or reporter) to ensure that all students are engaged in the activity. And providing students with hundred charts to record their ideas will support them as number logic problems increase in complexity.

Using a Venn Diagram to Organize Ideas

Venn diagrams are also helpful tools in sorting out the clues in logic problems. Consider this problem:

> **Kennedy Middle School is planning a sports banquet for members of their basketball, volleyball, and soccer teams. Seventeen students play each sport. However, four students play both basketball and volleyball; three play both basketball and soccer; five play volleyball and soccer, and three students play all 3 sports. How many students will be at the banquet?**

Students can use a Venn diagram to organize the data for this problem. The Venn diagram provides a way for students to visualize an otherwise confusing problem. Each of the circles can be labeled so that it represents students who play either basketball, volleyball, or soccer. The sections where two circles overlap represent students who play both sports, and the section where all three circles overlap represents students who play all three sports. Students can work with small manipulatives, pictures that represent players, or numerals to determine where each player belongs on the Venn diagram. Working in pairs will provide students with opportunities to experiment with ideas and talk about the reasons for their placement choices. As students see that they can place the five students who play all three sports in the center section where all three circles overlap, then place those who play two sports in the appropriate locations on the diagram, and then determine how many play only one sport, they are able to solve the problem (see Figure 9–4.)

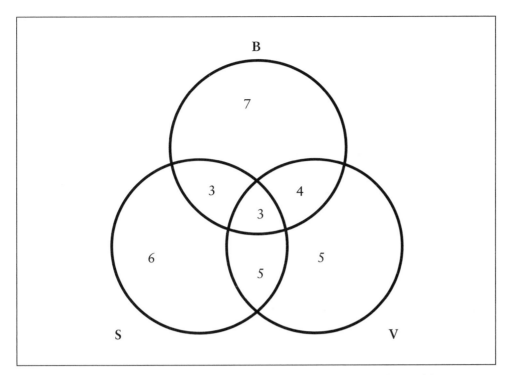

Figure 9–4 *Using a Venn diagram allows students to visualize the problem.*

Model your thoughts by speaking aloud as you solve logic problems with your students. Thinking is an abstract process, but through think-alouds and graphic organizers, you can help your students "see" logical thinking.

C L A S S R O O M - T E S T E D   T I P

Creating Matrix and Venn Diagram Problems

Recognizing problem situations that match certain problem-solving strategies will help students refine their thinking skills. Have students create some logical reasoning problems that fit with the use of a matrix. A matrix helps us sort out clues to find a one-on-one match. Have students work with partners to write a problem in which a matrix would be a reasonable tool. Model one together (i.e., 3 children and 3 toys with clues to figure out which child had which toy, or 4 men and 4 cars and clues to determine which car belonged to each man). Have each pair create their matrix and use it to solve their problem to be sure that the clues lead to a solution. Students can also write logical reasoning problems that might be solved with a Venn diagram (e.g., students who like rock music, students who like country music, students who like both, and students who like neither). Have them use a Venn diagram to show how their problem can be solved.

Communicating About the Strategy

Don't forget to have students write about and talk about how they solved logic problems. Try prompts like these:

▧ Explain the strategy you used to solve this problem.

▧ Explain why you set up your matrix or Venn diagram the way you did.

▧ Explain how the matrix or Venn diagram helped you solve the problem.

▧ How did recording and eliminating possibilities help you solve the problem?

▧ What was difficult about this problem? How did you make it easier?

Questions for Discussion

1. What is the importance of recording information when working on logical reasoning tasks?

2. How can teachers help students develop logic skills?

3. How does the use of lists, matrices, and Venn diagrams simplify logical reasoning tasks? How might students begin to recognize when each tool would be best used?

CHAPTER 10

Strategy: Work Backward

Strategies are learned over time, are applied in particular contexts, and become more refined, elaborate, and flexible as they are used in increasingly complex problem situations.

—National Council of Teachers of Mathematics,
Principles and Standards for School Mathematics

Working backward requires reversing our thinking. We work backward to solve a problem when we know how a situation ends, but we don't know how it started. In early grades we make it very concrete and simply ask students to "undo what was done" to get to an answer. By the middle grades, working backward can take the more abstract form of inverse operations.

Working backward problems can frustrate students in the middle grades because they generally contain unknown data at the beginning of the problem. Consider the following problem:

> **Mrs. Anderson went shopping to prepare for hurricane season. First, she spent half of her money on non-perishable food. Then she spent $23.94 on batteries, and then $25.80 on bottled water. She had $22.08 left. How much money did Mrs. Anderson have at the start?**

Knowing that Mrs. Anderson spent half her money is not particulary helpful if we do not know how much money she had prior to spending half. Half is an arbitrary amount, with half of 100 being different from half of 20 or half of 4. To find the solution, students will need to begin at the end of problem with information that is exact ($22.08) and then reverse the actions to find out how the situation began:

> *"We know she had $22.08. The last thing she did was spend $25.80 on bottled water, so let's say that she never spent that on water. Let's give her the $25.80 back. I'll add the $25.80 to the $22.08 she had and find that she had $47.88 before she bought water. If I also add back the $23.94 she spent for batteries, I find that she had $71.82 before she bought the batteries. Just before that she spent half of her money on food, so she must have spent $71.82 on food because that would be the other half. $71.82 × 2 = $143.64. She must have had $143.64 at the start!"*

A critical step in ensuring student success with this strategy is reminding students to routinely check the answer. Because students often become confused when reversing operations, a simple check will allow them to find their mistakes.

> *"Let's see if that works. If Mrs. Anderson had $143.64 and spent half of it on food, she would have had $71.82 left. If she then spent $25.80 on water and $23.94 on batteries, she would have $22.08 left. That matches the data in the problem! I was right!"*

Recognizing Familiar Problems

To help students determine when to apply this strategy, it is important that we provide opportunities for students to talk through their thought processes as they are deciding whether this strategy might be appropriate. Past problems that were discussed with the class are often used as reference points in class discussions. Consider this problem:

> Jenna bought some cookies for her party.
> She bought 9 fewer spice cookies than oatmeal.
> She bought the same number of oatmeal as peanut butter.
> She bought 5 less than twice as many peanut butter as chocolate chip.
> She bought 2 dozen chocolate chip cookies.
> How many cookies did Jenna buy?

While the problem may not initially look the same as the Hurricane Supplies problem, there are similarities that should be discussed. It is these similarities that offer a clue to how it might be solved. Through teacher questioning (e.g., What do we know at the start of the problem? How could we find out? What information does the problem give us?), students can recognize that, as in the Hurricane Supplies problem, knowing that Jenna bought 9 fewer spice cookies than oatmeal doesn't tell us how many spice cookies she bought until we know how many oatmeal cookies she bought.

As in the previous problem, students must begin with what they know and work backwards. They know that Jenna bought 2 dozen, or 24, chocolate chip. She bought 5 less than twice as many peanut butter, so she bought 5 less than 2 × 24, or 48 – 5 = 43 peanut butter. She bought the same number of oatmeal as peanut butter, so she bought 43 oatmeal. Nine fewer spice cookies than oatmeal would be 43 – 9 = 34. So, Jenna bought a total of 34 + 43 + 43 + 24 = 144 cookies. Working with terms like *same, 9 fewer, and 5 less than twice as many* will also help prepare students to use these terms when writing algebraic equations.

Preparing for Hurricane Season

Mrs. Anderson went shopping to prepare for hurricane season. First, she spent half of her money on non-perishable food. Then she spent $23.94 on batteries, and then $25.80 on bottled water. She had $22.08 left. How much did Mrs. Anderson have at the start?

Mrs. Anderson had $ 143.64 .

Show your work.

```
  22.08  left
  25.80  on water
+ 23.94  on batteries
 ───────
  71.82
 ×     2
 ───────
$143.64  total
         at
         start
 ───────
```

Explain how you solved this problem.

I worked backwards she had $22.08 left so I added all the money and multiplied it by 2 because it says at the begining that she spent half of it so I did the opposite and multiplied

Figure 10–1 *This student began with the amount that was left and worked backward.*

Preparing for Hurricane Season

Mrs. Anderson went shopping to prepare for hurricane season. First, she spent half of her money on non-perishable food. Then she spent $23.94 on batteries, and then $25.80 on bottled water. She had $22.08 left. How much did Mrs. Anderson have at the start?

Mrs. Anderson had ___143.64___ .

Show your work.

$$X \cdot \frac{1}{2} - 23.94 - 25.80 = 22.08$$
$$+25.80 \quad +25.80$$
$$X \cdot \frac{1}{2} - 23.94 = 47.88$$
$$+23.94 \quad +23.94$$
$$X \cdot \frac{1}{2} = 71.82$$
$$\overline{\quad \frac{1}{2} \quad}$$
$$X = 143.64$$

Explain how you solved this problem.

To solve this problem I used the strategy to work backwords. While solving the problem I added the charges to what she had left. Then, when left with x·½=71.82 I divided by .5 to get what x was.

Figure 10–2 *This student used a variable to represent the amount of money Mrs. Anderson had at the start, and then he wrote and solved an equation to find the answer.*

CLASSROOM-TESTED TIP

Working Backward: A Real-World Application

Have students keep a record of how long it takes them to get ready for school. They should keep track of how long it takes them to shower, get dressed, eat breakfast, and anything else that they typically do before school. They should also record how long it takes them to get to school. If they ride a bus, they can list the time the bus arrives at their bus stop. Once they know how much time they require to get ready for school, they can work backward from the school's starting time to determine what time they should be getting up in the morning. They can take this one step further to figure out what time they should be going to bed in order to get their required amount of sleep. This valuable life skill is an excellent application of the Work Backward strategy.

As an extension, students can write their own work-backward problems and pose them to classmates. For example, a student shared the following problem:

> *I get up at 5:52 a.m. It takes me 12 minutes to shower, 23 minutes to get dressed and dry my hair, 7 minutes to collect my books, lunch money, etc. I also eat breakfast before getting on the bus. The bus ride to school takes 24 minutes and arrives at school at 7:10 a.m. How much time do I spend eating breakfast?*

Students could solve this problem by starting with the school arrival time of 7:10 and working backward:

> *If you got to school at 7:10 and it took 24 minutes on the bus, you left home at 6:46. It took you 7 minutes to collect your stuff, 23 minutes to get dressed and dry your hair, and 12 minutes to shower. So 7 + 23 + 12 = 42. All of those things took a total of 42 minutes. If I subtract or go back 42 minutes from 6:46, that takes us back to 6:04. However, you got up at 5:52, so you must have spent the extra 12 minutes eating breakfast.*

It is important to help students in the middle grades make the connection between a Work Backward strategy and an algebraic representation of the same problem. Teachers can use a think-aloud to demonstrate an algebraic solution:

> *I want to figure out how much time you spent eating breakfast. I know that you got to school at 7:10 and you got up at 5:52, so you spent a total of 78 minutes getting ready and getting to school. If I use 'B' to represent the number of minutes spent eating breakfast, I could write the following equation:*

$$24 + 7 + 23 + 12 + B = 78$$
$$66 + B = 78$$
$$B = 12$$

> *When I subtract 66 minutes from the total 78 minutes, I can see that you spent 12 minutes eating breakfast.*

Increasing the Complexity of Problems

As students become proficient with working backward, we can increase the complexity of the task. This might be done by adding more complex numbers (e.g., larger numbers, fractions, decimals, percents) or by adding more criteria or changing the order of the information. Consider the following problem:

> **Caroline waited in line for the rides at the amusement park. She got on the log flume ride in $\frac{2}{3}$ the time that it took to wait in line for the roller coaster. The rapids ride wait was $\frac{3}{5}$ of the time it took to wait for the log flume. The spinner wait was $\frac{5}{6}$ of the time it took to wait for the rapids ride. Caroline waited in line $\frac{3}{4}$ hour for the roller coaster. How long was the wait for each ride?**

This problem is a work backward problem with added complexity. Fractions alone can complicate a problem, and these fractions relate to time rather than just being fractions of whole numbers. In addition, the order of the clues provides a challenge for even those students who recognize that they should work backward because after determining that Caroline stood in line for 45 minutes for the roller coaster, they move up to the next clues (the information on the waits for the spinner and rapids rides) and find no information that helps them continue through to the solution. Instead, they now have to move up to the first clue in the problem (She got on the log flume ride in $\frac{2}{3}$ the time that it took to wait in line for the roller coaster.) to find information that will allow them to continue. The order of the clues has been mixed up to challenge students to locate the appropriate information. In this problem, students need to first recognize that working backward makes sense as a strategy, and then have to apply the strategy, use appropriate computations related to fractions and time, and simplify the problem by reordering the clues. Discussions about what makes a problem easy or hard, or how students can simplify confusing problems, are important components of problem-solving instruction.

Students might also be challenged with problems that require them to use their measurement skills with a work-backward process. Rather than asking students to compute the volume of a box, consider posing a problem in which students have to work backward to find the height of the box, as in the following problem:

> **Miss Bronston has a box to store her classroom supplies. The volume of the box is 7371 cubic inches. The length of the box is 22.5 inches and the width is 16.8 inches. What is the height of the box?**

In order to solve the problem, students might begin with the knowledge that 7371 cubic inches represents the volume, or the length × width × height. They must first multiply length × width and then divide 7371 by that product to find the height. Since 22.5 inches × 16.8 inches = 378 square inches, students can divide 7371 cubic inches by 378 square inches to find that the height is 19.5 inches. By starting with the volume and working backward, students were able to find the missing data.

Working Backward with Equations

Another way to demonstrate working backward is to use equations. In order to solve an equation, we are "undoing" the order of operations. This reinforces the notion of using inverse operations to solve algebraic equations.

$$\underline{\hspace{2cm}} \times 3 - 1 = 11$$

In order to find the missing number, ask students to think about what was the last thing done according to the order of operations. They can then work backward, reversing the operations, to solve the problem.

> *"I have 11 now. The last thing done was subtraction, so I'll add one. Now I have 12. The next-to-last thing done was multiplication by 3, so I will divide by 3. Since 12 ÷ 3 = 4, I know that 4 should be the number I started with."*

Remember, a very important step in the Work Backward strategy is checking the answer by plugging it back into the problem and seeing if it works. Remind students to always do this.

$$4 \times 3 - 1 = 11 \quad \text{It works!}$$

CLASSROOM-TESTED TIP

Differentiating Instruction

Students within the same classroom often have varied experience and expertise with problem-solving strategies. It is important to present lessons that allow students to explore the strategy at different levels of complexity, depending on their needs. While all students might be involved in whole-class discussions about the Work Backward strategy, students can be grouped to allow some groups to explore more advanced tasks than others. Consider modifying problems for various groups to provide students with thought-provoking, but positive, experiences as they explore the strategy and refine their skills.

> *Beginning level*— Daniel bought a booklet of tickets for the carnival rides. He gave half of the tickets to Byron. Then he gave half of what he had left to Sharon. After that he had 6 tickets for himself. How many tickets were in the booklet that Daniel bought?

Developing level—Daniel bought a booklet of tickets for the carnival rides. He gave $\frac{1}{4}$ of the tickets to Byron. Then he gave half of what he had left to Sharon. After that he had 6 tickets for himself. How many tickets were in the booklet that Daniel bought?

Advanced level—Daniel bought a booklet of tickets for the carnival rides. He gave $\frac{1}{4}$ of the tickets to Byron. Then he gave $\frac{1}{3}$ of what he had left to Sharon. After that he had 6 tickets for himself. How many tickets were in the booklet that Daniel bought?

Posing problems at different levels will allow you to meet the needs of all learners within your classroom. The practice problems on the CD represent varying levels of complexity. Selecting problems, or modifying problems, to match the needs of your students will help them build their problem-solving skills. Other ideas for differentiating instruction for different levels of students include the following:

- Have an additional component to the problem for groups that complete the first step (e.g., Tickets cost $0.35 each. How much did Daniel pay for the booklet of tickets?).

- Vary the data in the second part of the problem to simplify or increase the complexity of the problem (i.e., Tickets cost $0.10 each—a simple computation, $0.35 each—a more difficult computation, or 2 for $0.45—involves some reasoning and computation).

- Allow students access to hands-on materials to "act out" the problem.

- Provide calculators to support students with the computations.

- While some groups work effectively on their own, others may need your input and guidance, or even some modeling, to better understand the process.

Note: Cooperative group work is a great way to help all students refine their problem-solving skills. Both homogeneous and heterogeneous groups are valuable instructional formats. Heterogeneous groups (students of varied ability levels) provide an opportunity for students of different levels to learn from each other and hear each other's insights. But homogeneous groups allow you to select problems of different difficulty levels and allow faster-moving groups to extend their skills, and slower-moving groups to explore activities that challenge, but do not frustrate, them. Provide students with opportunities to work in both homogeneous and heterogeneous groups as they work on refining their problem-solving skills.

Communicating About the Strategy

Be sure to have students write and talk about the strategy they used to solve the problem. Try prompts like these:

- How did working backward help you solve this problem?

- Explain to a friend, who has never tried this strategy, how to work backward to solve a problem.

- Why is working backward a good strategy for solving this problem?

- Why is it important to check your work after solving a problem using the Work Backward strategy?

- Write a problem that could be solved by working backward.

Questions for Discussion

1. Why do visual demonstrations or hand-on tasks help students better understand and remember strategies like working backward?

2. How might a teacher help students determine when working backward is a reasonable strategy to use to solve a problem?

3. How can an understanding of working backward support students when they are solving equations in algebra?

4. In what ways can teachers continue to challenge students as they develop their work-backward skills? How might problems be made more complex?

CHAPTER 11

Assessing Problem Solving

Assessment should not merely be done to students; rather it should also be done for students, to guide and enhance their learning.

—National Council of Teachers of Mathematics,
Principles and Standards for School Mathematics

The Role of Ongoing Assessment

Teachers have traditionally viewed assessment as a culminating activity, providing information about whether each student has mastered a unit's content. Fortunately, we are beginning to recognize that assessment must take place throughout the instructional process. Ongoing assessment allows us to gather information about students' learning and monitor students' progress. It also helps us make sound instructional decisions by identifying those skills and concepts that need to be retaught or modified to ensure success for all students. Rather than being a final wrap-up of what was learned, assessment should guide our instruction to ensure that we are on track with our instructional activities. A thorough understanding of problem-solving assessment will guide you as you plan solid instructional activities that specifically address your assessment outcomes.

Because of the value of ongoing assessment in guiding the instructional process, it is critical that assessment and instruction be developed hand in hand. Consider our mathematics outcomes as our travel destination. Without a clear view of our students' destination, it will be difficult to determine the path they should travel to get there. But, with expected student outcomes in mind, instructional activities can be designed to move our students in the direction of their destination. Frequent assessment activities will ensure that our students stay on the right path and will help redirect those students who might become lost along the way.

During instruction, students explore and practice their skills under the guidance and direction of the teacher. Informal assessment should occur during instruction as teachers observe students at work, listen to their discussions, and question to check their understanding. During formal assessment, however, students are given opportunities to solve problems without teacher support. Problem solving may happen in groups or individually, but it happens without teacher guidance. These independent tasks provide an idea of how each student is progressing in his or her skill development. They provide information that will be essential for planning subsequent classroom lessons or valuable to share during individual student or parent conferences. Both informal and formal assessments allow us to analyze students' work for patterns in errors or clues to misunderstandings about the concepts we've taught.

In assessing problem solving, attention should be paid to both the process and the product. When analyzing students' problem-solving abilities, some very helpful types of assessment are teacher observations of the problem-solving process, interviews with students, and the evaluation of written, open-ended problem-solving tasks. By analyzing both student behaviors and the products created during their problem-solving experiences, we can gather a wealth of information to assess our students' problem-solving abilities and plan for future instruction.

Finally, it is important to recognize that what we think we have taught is not always what students have learned. Despite our belief that a concept was fully explained

Figure 11–1 *Listening to students explain their thinking is an invaluable way to assess their understanding.*

or a process was sufficiently modeled, if students are still confused, it is our responsibility to think of new ways to address it until they have learned it. Ongoing assessment helps us determine when clarification, revision, or reteaching is appropriate.

The Value of Observations

Much information can be gained about students' understanding of the problem-solving process through classroom observations. As students solve problems in pairs or groups, the teacher should circulate throughout the classroom, assessing students' understanding of the process. By listening to group discussions, the teacher can gather valuable information regarding students' understanding of the problem, their ability to work together and share ideas as they work toward a solution, and their ability to judge the reasonableness of both their plan and, ultimately, their solution. As students explain their ideas to other group members or challenge others' thinking, we gather information about each student's level of expertise. These observations can be informal and used simply to get a general sense of class abilities, or they can be formal observations in which checklists are used to evaluate individual students or groups of students. Teacher-developed checklists help us gather information on students' ability to collaborate, reason, and problem solve. You will find a Problem-Solving Group Observation Checklist on the CD.

Observation checklists may also be designed for individual student assessment. Checklist items might include whether a specific student contributed to the problem-solving activity, was able to restate a problem or explain a solution, or contributed a reasonable strategy to the group's discussion. Whether observations are formal or informal, they provide insight into students' understanding of the problem-solving process. Post-observation conferences with individuals or groups allow us to discuss our observations with students and help them see the value of collaborative problem solving.

The Value of Interviews

Student interviews provide tremendous insight into students' problem-solving skills. In talking with individual students about a specific problem-solving task, the teacher gains an understanding of the student's thinking as he or she approached the task. Interviews allow us to ask questions like "Why did you decide to do that?", "Did you have any difficulties as you were trying to solve this problem?", or "Was there any other way you could have solved this?" Interviews provide us with the background information to understand what we see on a student's paper.

Interviews can be formal or informal. Some teachers like to set up formal conferences. As the class is working on a task, individual students are asked to meet with the teacher for a brief conference. With their papers in hand, students are asked to explain, justify, or describe their thinking. Informal conferences also provide valuable information. As students are working on problem-solving activities, the teacher might pull a chair up to a pair or an individual student and ask some probing questions to better understand their thinking. Whether formal or informal, interviews with students can shed light on their understanding of the problem-solving process.

The Value of Rubrics in Assessment

Written assessment tasks provide information on individual students' problem-solving abilities. While multiple-choice tests may be appropriate in some mathematical situations, open-ended assignments provide much more information when assessing problem solving. Students' responses to open-ended problem situations provide us with valuable information about their level of understanding of the problem-solving process.

To be most effective, scoring keys should be developed before instruction takes place. In this way, we can focus on what we want students to learn and then design instructional tasks that will get them there. A general scoring key that can be applied to a set of activities is called a *rubric*. The use of rubrics to assess problem-solving activities offers students a chance to see what is expected of them before they begin a problem-solving task. It can help guide them as they work through a problem, reminding them of the important points to consider in solving the problem. After their task is scored, it allows them to see the degree to which they were able to meet the assessment criteria, and therefore, it becomes a valuable tool in helping them understand how they can improve their work.

A Holistic Rubric for Problem Solving

A holistic rubric rates the student's ability to complete a task that is a compilation of several outcomes. Problem solving is such a task. There are several key outcomes that we look for when assessing students' problem-solving skills.

First, students should be able to select and use an appropriate strategy. Not all students will select the same strategy, but each selection should make sense as a means to solve the problem (see Figure 11–2).

Second, students should be able to find a correct solution. There may be more than one correct solution. Students' solutions need to make sense with the data they have at hand. In addition, students' answers need to be the result of correct calculations.

Third, students need to be able to communicate about their problem solving. Our students' abilities to communicate their thoughts about solving problems provide us with a clearer picture of each student's level of knowledge. Their writing offers insight into the process they went through to arrive at their answer. It often provides information about which we might otherwise need to conjecture. In light of the strong emphasis of the NCTM Standards regarding the development of mathematical communication, it is recommended that writing be integrated into the problem-solving process and become a part of the holistic rubric.

Once teachers have set outcomes for their students, developing a problem-solving rubric becomes easy. As students look at their completed problems, they are able to see the outcomes they have met and those that they have not yet mastered. With

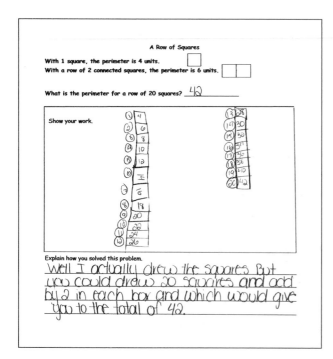

Figure 11–2 *Student A uses a drawing and student B explores number patterns to find solutions to the same problem. Note how student A's drawing led her to discover another strategy, the use of patterns, for solving the problem.*

this information in mind, they become able to revise their work to move closer to exemplary quality work.

Figure 11–3 is a holistic rubric for problem-solving activities. First, the rubric lists the expected student outcomes, and then it outlines the criteria needed to earn scores ranging from 0 to 4.

This rubric offers a quick and easy way to assess our students' ability to solve problems. In this rubric, selection of an appropriate strategy, calculation of a correct answer, and an effective explanation of the answer are the expected student outcomes. The ultimate goal is that students are able to meet all three outcomes as a demonstration of their problem-solving skills. Students who have seen the rubric prior to the activity will be focused on these three important outcomes that they are expected to demonstrate. In this way, the rubric helps guide students through the problem-solving experience.

In order to score a 2 or higher, students must demonstrate their ability to select and use an appropriate strategy. Selecting a reasonable strategy is the foundation for good problem solving. If a student lacks the ability to think through a situation and decide on a plan for solving the problem, his or her correct answer may be no more than a lucky guess. Students who are also able to find a correct answer based on an appropriate strategy and explain the strategy they selected will receive higher scores to correlate with their greater ability to complete the problem-solving task.

While the first two expected outcomes (selecting an appropriate strategy and calculating a correct answer) will always remain the same, the final outcome may be re-

Expected Student Outcomes:

Students will be able to

1. select and use an appropriate strategy.

2. calculate a correct answer.

3. explain their strategy for solving the problem.

Problem-Solving Rubric:

4 – arrived at a correct answer; used an appropriate strategy; adequately explained answer

3 – used an appropriate strategy; calculated a correct answer but was unable to explain the strategy; or adequately explained the strategy but did not calculate a correct answer

2 – used an appropriate strategy; did not find a correct answer; could not explain the strategy

1 – attempted to solve the problem, but completely incorrect in attempt

0 – no attempt/blank

Figure 11–3 *Rubrics are designed with expected student outcomes in mind.*

worded to direct students to different types of mathematical communication. Some examples might include justifying the solution or explaining why a particular strategy was used. In each case, the outcome of strengthening mathematical communication is addressed with a slightly different writing assignment.

The Role of Rubrics in Improvement

The rubric is an effective tool for guiding students in revising their problem solving. Many teachers allow students to rewrite responses after the initial scoring. This technique encourages students to focus on the rubric and attempt to improve their writing and increase their score. Much as a revision checklist helps students polish a written composition in language arts class, the rubric guides students in their mathematical revision process.

Evaluating My Problem Solving, which is included on the CD, will direct students through an analysis of their work. As students review their own work with the rubric in mind, they are able to see ways in which they can improve. The ability of students to analyze and improve their own work is our ultimate goal, as it indicates that students have internalized the strategies we have taught.

You can assist students in strengthening their problem-solving abilities and developing their writing skills in several ways. Think-alouds that model well-developed explanations provide students with examples of logical thinking. And discussions among partners or groups, during which students can share their ideas, help students develop a variety of ways to explain their thinking process.

Problem solving is a thinking skill. In order to monitor how students' thinking is progressing, it is important to frequently ask students to share their thoughts both orally and in writing. Students' writing allows us to recognize difficulties or misunderstandings they might be experiencing. It offers a valuable glimpse into their thinking processes and allows us to determine if they are progressing smoothly in their understanding of the problem-solving process.

Self-Reflections on Problem Solving

Teachers should offer students opportunities to reflect on their problem solving through journal writing, allowing them to express their successes and frustrations as they develop as problem solvers. Problem-solving journals that allow students to reflect on daily or weekly lessons provide us with insight into our students' perceptions, confusions, and successes. See Reflecting on Problem Solving on the CD for ideas for open-ended journal writing prompts. Reflective writing should not be scored, although teacher comments are recommended. Teacher/student dialogues can begin through journal writing in which we encourage our students and point out their growth and successes.

Varied Assessment

Rubrics are a valuable way to analyze students' progress. Teacher observations, student interviews, and student self-reflections also contribute important data to the assessment process. Ongoing and varied assessment throughout the teaching process will provide the information we need to make strong instructional decisions and, ultimately, create a classroom filled with successful problem solvers.

C L A S S R O O M · T E S T E D · T I P

**Using Rubrics to Improve Mathematical
Communication Skills**

One way to help students see the degree to which an explanation is clear and detailed is to evaluate writing samples as a class. Write several responses of your own, with varying degrees of clarity, and have students score them using the rubric. Teachers can provide students with 5 index cards numbered 0–4. Students can then raise the index card that shows the score they would give each writing sample. As students give a score to the writing sample, have them justify the score using the criteria in the scoring key. Together, the class can rewrite the sample to give it a higher score.

Mathematical Communication Rubric Expected Student Outcome:

Students will be able to clearly explain the strategy they used to solve the problem.

Rubric:

4 exemplary explanation; detailed and clear; may have provided examples
3 explanation contained adequate details; adequate clarity
2 explanation somewhat clear; lacks details
1 attempted an explanation, but incorrect or unclear
0 no attempt = blank

Another technique that helps students learn to use a rubric to guide revision is compiling a list of responses with scores of 1, 2, 3, and 4. In pairs or groups, the students discuss and evaluate the differences between the writing samples and attempt to determine what is missing in the responses that scored 1, 2, and 3. Together, each group works to rewrite the 1 to make it a 2 or better, the 2 to make it a 3 or better, or the 3 to make it a 4. Groups can then present their revised writing to the class. Showing students concrete examples of how to improve their writing with details, examples, and clarity of thought will help them strengthen their skills in communicating about their math thinking.

Questions for Discussion

1. Why is problem solving frequently scored using a rubric rather than simply by the correct answer?

2. What can teachers learn through students' communication about their problem solving?

3. What does it mean to say that we assess both product and process during problem-solving instruction?

12

Problem Solving Across the Content Standards

The kinds of experiences teachers provide clearly play a major role in determining the extent and quality of students' learning.

—National Council of Teachers of Mathematics,
Principles and Standards for School Mathematics

Problem solving is a critical process skill, but it does not stand alone. It is connected to other processes through which students learn and explore math ideas. The NCTM Process Standards (2000) of problem solving, communication, representation, reasoning and proof, and connections describe critical processes that are intertwined in our math lessons. As they solve problems, students communicate verbally and in writing in order to process and express their ideas. They decipher representations to understand problem data or create representations to show their thinking. They use reasoning skills to make inferences, draw conclusions, and justify their solutions. They connect various math ideas in order to better understand each one, and they connect math to their lives as they explore problems in a real-world context. These five process standards interconnect in daily lessons as we develop and refine math content with our students.

Although there is much overlap between the process standards, there must also be a strong connection between the process and content standards. Problem solving is a process through which students learn math content and through which they are able to apply their math skills. Providing students with experiences solving problems in various content areas is a critical way to help students practice applying these skills as well as actively engaging them with math content. The National Council of Teachers of Mathematics (2000) has outlined the content standards for middle grades students and has organized those standards in five content areas: number and operations, algebra, measurement, geometry, and data analysis and probability. As we help students develop their skills in the processes of problem solving, reasoning and proof, communication, representation, and connections, we also focus on building their understanding of this content.

Problem Solving About Number and Operations

Students in grades 6 through 8 are continuing to explore relationships between numbers and the ways in which numbers are represented. They are expected to understand how to use fractions to solve problems. In addition, they are developing their understanding of the meanings and effects of arithmetic operations (addition, subtraction, multiplication, division) with fractions and decimals.

The Problem Task

In the following lesson, eighth graders were engaged in exploring their understanding of fractions through a partner problem-solving task.

> Stefanie ate $\frac{3}{8}$ of a pizza. Later she got hungry and ate $\frac{1}{2}$ of what was left. How much of the pizza is still left?

To promote discussion about their thinking, eighth-grade students were asked to work in pairs or small groups to solve this problem. The teacher, Mrs. Boyer, posed the problem and clarified the task by asking students if they thought that they would be able to find the answer to the problem in one step. The class agreed that this was a multi-step problem. Mrs. Boyer then asked the class to identify some questions that would need to be answered in solving this problem. She recorded their suggestions on the board. The class agreed that they would probably need to find answers to the following questions:

■ How much pizza was left after Stefanie's first meal?

■ How much did Stefanie eat the second time?

■ How much did she eat altogether?

■ How much was left?

Next, Mrs. Boyer reviewed the different problem-solving strategies and asked students to think about which strategies they might use to solve this problem. She then asked students to solve the problem with their partners, recording their work, solutions, and explanations of how they solved the problem. Students had access to paper, pencils, and calculators. Mrs. Boyer moved through the room to monitor and support students as they worked (a benefit of partner and group work is the teacher's freedom to move to different groups and question or support them as needed).

A first step for many of the students was to visualize the problem situation. Students created pictures to represent the pizza, ranging from round pizzas to rectangular pizzas. Those students who used a picture began by dividing their "pizzas" into eighths and then shading three of the eight pieces to represent the portion of the pizza that Stefanie ate the first time. The students were then able to use their diagrams to determine that when Stefanie ate $\frac{1}{2}$ of the remaining five pieces, she had two-and-a-half pieces of pizza left.

Many students thought that they had found the solution—two-and-a-half pieces of pizza were left! However, Mrs. Boyer told them that they still had to determine what part of the pizza was left. Several students said that two-and-a-half pieces could be represented by the fraction

$$\frac{2\frac{1}{2}}{8}$$

since the pizza was divided into eighths. They knew that this fraction could be simplified, and some multiplied the complex fraction by $\frac{2}{2}$ to get $\frac{5}{16}$. Others used their diagram to resolve this issue. They realized that if they cut each piece of pizza in half, they would have a total of sixteen pieces. Stefanie would have eaten six pieces originally, then five of the remaining ten pieces. That would leave five pieces or $\frac{5}{16}$ of the pizza.

Although most of the students used fractions to solve the problem, Stephen and Ramon converted the fractions to decimals. These students did not use a diagram. Instead, they used a calculator to convert $\frac{3}{8}$ to 0.375. They then subtracted 0.375 from 1 to get 0.625, the amount of pizza left after Stefanie's first meal. Next, they multiplied 0.625 by 0.5 to determine how much pizza Stefanie ate the second time. They then subtracted that amount, 0.3125, from 0.625 to find that 0.3125 still remained. Mrs. Boyer asked them how they could check their answer. Stephen said that he knew that there were 2.5 pieces of pizza left, so that would mean $\frac{2.5}{8}$ of the pizza. He then used his calculator to divide 2.5 by 8 to verify his answer of 0.3125.

In order to differentiate instruction, Mrs. Boyer provided a second-tier challenge problem to students or groups as they finished the first problem, allowing students to work at their own pace to solve the main problem while providing those who had finished an extension problem to solve. She asked each student to justify his or her solution to the original problem, and those who were able to explain their thinking in a manner that demonstrated conceptual understanding were given the following challenge problem.

If Stefanie's brother ate $\frac{1}{5}$ of what was left, how much pizza now remains?

Four students or groups completed the bonus problem. Three of them used a diagram of the pizza. These diagrams showed the students' solutions to the original problem, with the pizza divided into sixteenths and five pieces remaining. These students then explained that if Stefanie's brother ate $\frac{1}{5}$ of the remaining five pieces, that left four pieces, or $\frac{4}{16}$ of the pizza. Stephen again converted fractions to decimals. He converted $\frac{1}{5}$ to 0.2 and then multiplied 0.2 by his previous result, 0.3125, to get

Stefanie's Pizza

Stefanie ate 3/8 of a pizza. Later she got hungry and ate 1/2 of what was left. How much of the pizza is still left?

Show your work.

So theres 5 pieces left.

So she has 2½ pieces left

Then I divide the whole thing into sixteenths and got $\frac{5}{16}$

Explain how you solved the problem.

First I drew 8 boxes to represent the pizza. The shaded 3 for the 3 she ate first. Then I found that there was 5 left then I drew the same box and shaded 3 along with half of what was left over. And got 2½ pieces. Then I divided the box and got 16 boxes all together, with 5 left. So I got $\frac{5}{16}$.

Figure 12–1 *This student drew a picture to represent the pizza as a rectangle.*

0.0625, the amount that Stefanie's brother ate. He then subtracted that from the remaining pizza, 0.3125, to get 0.25. Although most of the students benefited from using fractions and diagrams, Stephen was able to make sense of both parts of the problem by using decimals.

About the Math

This problem challenged students to combine their understanding of numbers and operations with their problem-solving skills. In solving this problem, students used their understanding of fractions as they determined eighths and sixteenths of a whole.

Stefanie's Pizza

Stefanie ate 3/8 of a pizza. Later she got hungry and ate 1/2 of what was left. How much of the pizza is still left?

_____

Show your work.

$8/8 = 1$
$3/8 = .375$
$5/8 = .625$

$\dfrac{8}{8} - \dfrac{3}{8} = 5/8$

$1 - .375 = .625$

$.625 \cdot .5 = .3125$

$.625 - .3125 = .3125$

After Stefanie ate her 2nd meal she had .3125 or 2.5/8 slices left.

Explain how you solved the problem.

I had to change the fractions into decimals because it was easier to work with. First, I had subtracted 3/8 from a full 8/8. I then got 5/8. at this point I had turned everything to decimals. I then found 1/2 of 5/8 and subtracted that from 5/8 and got .3125.

Figure 12–2 *This student converted fractions to decimals and chose appropriate operations to solve this multi-step problem.*

Some students demonstrated their understanding by drawing pictures to represent three-eighths of the whole and then dividing the remaining five-eighths into two equal parts. Others were able to convert fractions to decimals and then apply their recognition that finding one-half of the remaining pizza was equivalent to multiplying that quantity by 0.5. They then had to subtract to determine how much pizza was left. This involved a series of operations: first converting a fraction to a decimal, then subtracting that decimal from one whole, then multiplying the remaining pizza by 0.5, and then subtracting that quantity to find how much pizza was left.

As students strengthened their understanding of fractions and operations throughout this activity, they also refined their use of problem-solving strategies. Some students demonstrated their problem-solving skills as they created pictures and diagrams to simplify the problem, or they chose a correct operation as they added, subtracted, multiplied, or divided to get their answers. They continued to develop their skills at multistep problems as they proceeded through several steps in search of the answer. And they worked to enhance their problem-solving attitudes through persistence, despite some frustration, and cooperation with their partners as they worked together to share ideas and strategies.

This activity required students to pull from their understanding of fractions and operations to solve a multi-step problem. There were several effective methods for solving the problem, and students had opportunities to share their ideas and approaches with each other in order to expand their repertoire of problem-solving skills and enhance their understanding of fractions. Some students applied an already developed understanding of fractions and operations to the problem, while others gained insights and continued to refine their understandings through the problem-solving task. The teacher ensured that all students were engaged and challenged by asking students to defend their answer to the first problem and then posing a bonus problem for those who needed it.

Problem Solving About Algebra

An important algebraic goal for students in grades 6 through 8 is the strengthening of their understanding of patterns and functions. Students who can organize data to recognize patterns and discover relationships are better able to find solutions to problems. Representing and analyzing change in various contexts is an important algebra skill that develops as students observe change and attempt to determine how change in one variable relates to change in another. Describing this change and making generalizations about it are beneficial skills.

The Problem Task

The teacher, Mr. Gonzalez, posed the following problem to his eighth-grade class:

> **Sammy's Bicycle Shop sells bicycles and tricycles. Clarence went to Sammy's and counted 37 sets of handlebars and 95 wheels. How many bicycles and tricycles did Sammy have in his shop?**

After reading the problem, Mr. Gonzalez began by asking the class the following key questions to get them thinking:

- How many wheels does each bicycle have?

- How many wheels does each tricycle have?

■ How many sets of handlebars does each bicycle have?

■ How many sets of handlebars does each tricycle have?

He then reminded students about the different problem-solving strategies they had learned by displaying each of the strategy icons and asking students if they thought each strategy could possibly be used for solving this problem. As he went through the strategies one by one, students agreed that nearly every strategy could be useful for this problem.

Through small-group discussions, some students soon realized that if there were 37 sets of handlebars, there was also a total of 37 bicycles and tricycles. A few chose to work independently, but most worked with partners to determine how many of the 37 were bicycles and how many were tricycles. Many students used the Guess, Check, and Revise strategy. Some began by dividing 95 wheels by 5, the total number of wheels for one bicycle and one tricycle. This gave them a starting point of 19 bicycles and 19 tricycles. When they added $19 \times 2 = 38$ and $19 \times 3 = 57$, they got a total of 95 wheels and were convinced that they had solved the problem. Mr. Gonzalez then asked them how many sets of handlebars 19 bikes and 19 tricycles would have. Students quickly realized that they would have 38 sets of handlebars, not 37. Mr. Gonzalez encouraged these students to use their results to help them find another combination that would give both the correct numbers of wheels and sets of handlebars.

Some students were not sure how to begin solving the problem. After giving them a few minutes to discuss it with their partners, Mr. Gonzalez again referred them to the strategy icons and suggested that they might consider drawing a picture or making an organized list to help them keep track of their thoughts. With this hint, several students quickly began drawing 37 sets of handlebars to represent the total number of bicycles and tricycles. They then started adding either 2 or 3 wheels to each. Others seemed to be getting frustrated. In order to get them started, Mr. Gonzalez asked, "How could you draw a picture? Would you start by drawing the sets of handlebars or the wheels?" Bryan responded that they should start with the sets of handlebars because that's how many total bikes and tricycles they have. Once Bryan and his teammate drew the 37 sets of handlebars, they realized that they needed to figure out where to put the 95 wheels so that some would have two wheels and the remainder would have three wheels.

Once everyone had finished the problem, a whole-class sharing provided students with opportunities to describe their strategies and defend their answers. Mr. Gonzalez asked Abby to explain her solution to the class. She explained that she had actually used two strategies: Guess, Check, and Revise and Draw a Picture or Diagram. She used the drawing to help her visualize the bicycles and tricycles as she rearranged the wheels to find the right combination of 21 tricycles and 16 bicycles. Sean explained that he and his partner had started with the combination of $20 + 17 = 37$ sets of handlebars. They then multiplied $20 \times 3 = 60$ and $17 \times 2 = 34$. When they added $60 + 34 = 94$, they realized that they were very close. They then made the adjustment to 21 tricycles and 16 bicycles to give a total of $63 + 32 = 95$ wheels. They agreed when Mr. Gonzalez pointed out that they were very lucky to have begun with a guess that was so close!

Sammy's Bike Shop

Sammy's Bicycle Shop sells bicycles and tricycles. Clarence went to Sammy's and counted 37 handlebars and 95 wheels. How many bicycles and tricycles did Sammy have in his shop?

Guess, Check, and Revise

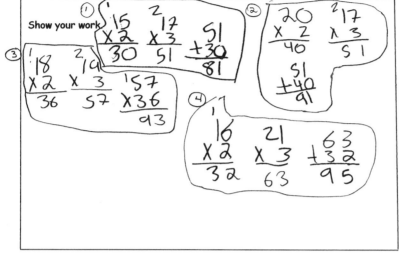

Explain how you solved the problem.

well first I tried three diffrent problems out but none of them work. So then I tried one more time and it came out as the answer.

Figure 12–3 *Although this student's first guess did not reflect the correct number of sets of handlebars, he was able to check and revise his second and third guesses effectively.*

Bryan shared the drawing strategy that he and his teammate had discovered. They drew 37 sets of handlebars, just as some of the other students had done. Next, they determined that these sets of handlebars could have either two or three wheels, so two was the minimum number of wheels for each. Bryan then drew two wheels for each handlebar set and showed the class that this used a total of 74 wheels. Then Bryan and his teammate agreed that they needed 95 − 74 = 21 more wheels. Bryan then drew an additional wheel onto 21 of the sets of handlebars, counting on from 74 as he did so, until he reached 95 wheels. There were "OH"s and "AH"s as students

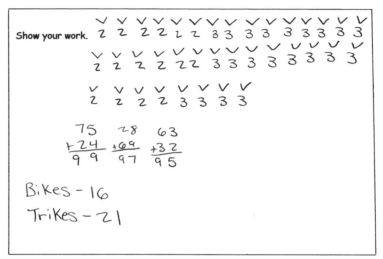

Sammy's Bike Shop

Sammy's Bicycle Shop sells bicycles and tricycles. Clarence went to Sammy's and counted 37 handlebars and 95 wheels. How many bicycles and tricycles did Sammy have in his shop?

Show your work.

75   28   63
+24   +69   +32
 99   97   95

Bikes - 16
Trikes - 21

Explain how you solved the problem.

I drew 37 v's to represent the handle bars then I guessed how many may be bikes and how many are trikes. I kept subtracting multiplying and adding until I came up with 95 wheels

Figure 12–4 *This student used a diagram to help visualize as she guessed, checked, and revised to find the solution.*

realized that this represented the 21 tricycles. The remaining handlebars with two wheels represented the 16 bicycles.

Mr. Gonzalez used this opportunity to connect students' solution strategies to the use of algebraic equations.

Mr. Gonzalez: How many wheels do 5 bicycles have?
Student: 10 wheels.
Mr. Gonzalez: How many wheels do 12 bicycles have?

STUDENT: 24 wheels.

MR. GONZALEZ: What if we didn't know how many bicycles we had? What if we used the variable *B* to represent the number of bicycles we had? How many wheels would *B* bicycles have?

STUDENT: 2*B* wheels, because each bicycle has 2 wheels.

MR. GONZALEZ: How many wheels do 5 tricycles have?

STUDENT: Each tricycle has 3 wheels, so 5 tricycles would have 15 wheels.

MR. GONZALEZ: If we use the variable *T* to represent the number of tricycles, how many wheels would *T* tricycles have?

STUDENT: 3*T*.

Mr. Gonzalez wrote the following on the board: $2B + 3T =$

MR. GONZALEZ: What do we know about $2B + 3T$?

STUDENT: It's the number of wheels on the bicycles plus the number of wheels on the tricycles.

STUDENT: It's the total number of wheels.

STUDENT: It has to equal 95.

(Mr. Gonzalez completed the equation written on the board: $2B + 3T = 95$.)

MR. GONZALEZ: Can we write another equation involving *B* and *T*? Remember that *B* represents the number of bicycles and *T* represents the number of tricycles.

STUDENT: We know that $B + T = 37$.

Figure 12–5 *This student is sharing an alternate solution strategy.*

Modeling problem situations with diagrams and recording and using data to make revisions are important skills for students in grades 6 through 8. These students are learning or will soon learn to solve a problem like this using algebra. Although none of his students had solved this problem algebraically, Mr. Gonzalez used their solution strategies to connect their thinking to algebraic equations. This problem could have been solved using either one variable or a system of two variables. For example, using one variable, if T represents the number of tricycles, then $(37 - T)$ would represent the number of bicycles. The following equation would represent the total number of wheels:

$$3T + 2(37 - T) = 95$$

Solving the equation, we see that $3T + 74 - 2T = 95$.
Therefore, $T = 21$ tricycles and $37 - 21 = 16$ bicycles.

A major focus of this task was the recognition and understanding that the number of bicycles (B) plus the number of tricycles (T) must total 37 and that the number of wheels on the bicycles ($2B$) plus the number of wheels on the tricycles ($3T$) must total 95. Without using formal algebraic equations, students were actually solving and making sense of the following system of equations:

$$B + T = 37$$
$$2B + 3T = 95$$

Problems like this one provide an important foundation for developing conceptual understanding of algebra. As students begin approaching problems by writing and solving equations, they will have a better understanding of why they use variables and what the variables represent.

Varied problem-solving strategies were noted during this task. Although most students used a variation of Guess, Check, and Revise to make sense of the problem, they used several different methods for choosing their initial guesses. As they refined their guesses based on the results of their checking, some looked for patterns as the number of bicycles increased and the number of tricycles decreased. Others used pictures or diagrams of sets of handlebars with either two or three wheels attached to each to help visualize their guessing and checking. With this combination of strategies, checking was simply a matter of counting wheels. As they shared their strategies with their partners and then with the whole class, students realized that there were many different ways to approach the problem.

Exploring ideas in a problem context engaged students and set the stage for student discovery about number sense and patterns. Allowing students the opportunity to discuss the problem with their partners and strategize about where to begin helped them form a foundation for using variables and writing equations and systems of equations. By having students share their solution strategies, the teacher enabled students to see that there were many different ways to approach and make sense of the problem. He then used this opportunity to bridge the conceptual foundation of students' strategies to the use of algebraic equations.

Problem Solving About Measurement

Students in grades 6 through 8 are expected to understand, select, and use appropriate units to measure attributes including perimeter and area. Although they are familiar with formulas and how to apply the formulas to calculate area and perimeter of rectangles, it is critical at this level that students recognize the concepts of area and perimeter in problem situations. In the following problem, students were challenged to demonstrate their understanding of area and perimeter as well as their ability to correctly calculate each.

The Problem Task

Seventh-grade students worked with partners to explore the following problem.

> **Mark has 64 square feet of grass sod to make a fenced-in playpen for his new puppy. What are some possible rectangles that he could make with the sod? Which one will require the least amount of fencing?**

Before they began, their teacher, Ms. Friedman, reviewed the properties of rectangles and other mathematical concepts students would need to solve this problem. She began by asking, "What are the properties of a rectangle?" One student said that opposite sides have to be equal. Ms. Friedman then drew a parallelogram on the whiteboard and asked if opposite sides were equal. Students agreed that they were, but that this was not a rectangle. Ms. Friedman then asked what else the parallelogram needed in order to be a rectangle, and another student responded that it needed four right angles. Ms. Friedman wanted to make sure that students realized that a square was also a rectangle. She drew several examples, including a square, as well as non-examples of rectangles, and asked students to identify which were rectangles. She then asked the students what 1 square foot of sod would look like. Lisa responded that it would look like a piece of grass that was square in shape and measured 1 foot on each side. Ms. Friedman agreed and explained that their task was to determine how to use the 64 square feet of sod.

At this point, Ms. Friedman began circulating around the room as pairs and small groups of students started working on the problem. Ms. Friedman reminded students that the different strategies and their icons would remain on the overhead projector in case they needed to refer back to them. Nearly every student began by drawing rectangles and trying to determine factors of 64.

Patrick called Ms. Friedman over to where he and his partner were working and asked, "Can it be 16 × 4?" Ms. Friedman verified that this was one way that Mark could construct his fenced-in playpen, but she asked, "Is that the only way he could do it? Patrick said that he wasn't sure, so Ms. Friedman suggested that he and his partner explore to see if they could find more options.

Ali showed Ms. Friedman a drawing of a rectangle that was 14 x 18. She asked if this was one of the possible rectangles that Mark could use in the problem. Ms. Friedman asked, "How many square feet of sod would that rectangle use?" Ali replied that it would use 64 square feet. When Ms. Friedman asked Ali how she got her answer, Ali replied that she had added 14 + 18 + 14 + 18 = 64. Ms. Friedman then asked Ali how many feet of fencing this rectangle would need. After doing some calculations, Ali responded that it would need 64 feet of fencing. When Ms. Friedman asked, "What did you find there, area or perimeter?" she heard a loud "OHHHH-HHH!!!!!!!!" as Ali realized that she had confused area and perimeter.

One group told Ms. Friedman that they believed they had found all possible rectangles. They had drawn rectangles that were 2×32, 4×16, and 8×8. Ms. Friedman asked them why they had chosen these side lengths. They explained that they had found the factors of 64: 2, 4, 8, 16, and 32. Ms. Friedman then asked what number was a factor of every number. All three students responded in unison, "ONE!" They then added 1×64 to their diagram.

Christina asked if the sides of the playpen had to be whole numbers. Ms. Friedman pointed out that the problem did not specify this, so Christina could try to find rectangles with side lengths that were not whole numbers if she wished. Christina had realized that a rectangle with dimensions $10\frac{2}{3} \times 6$ had an area of 64 square feet. However, she had used a decimal and had rounded it to 10.7. When she multiplied 10.7×6, she was getting an area of 64.2 square feet. Ms. Friedman suggested that Christina use the mixed numeral instead of rounding the decimal. That way she could be sure when comparing how much fencing was needed. Although Ms. Friedman had expected students to only consider whole numbers, she was thrilled that two or three students worked hard to find some dimensions that were not whole numbers.

As Ms. Friedman observed different pairs of students working together, she realized that several of them seemed to believe that they had finished the problem once they found all the possible dimensions for the playpen. She then reminded the class that they were being asked to determine two things: the possible rectangles for the playpen and which rectangle required the least amount of fencing. She added, "When you say which one requires the least amount of fencing, don't forget to explain how you know that." With this reminder, students went back to work to finish the problem.

During the whole-group discussion that followed, several students volunteered to share their solution strategies with the class. Ms. Friedman asked each to explain what they had done to solve the problem. Amy put her paper under the document camera and explained that she had divided 64 by 1, then by 2, then she tried to divide by 3, and she continued this process to find as many numbers as she could that "came out even." Then she "added up all the sides." Ms. Friedman wanted to be sure that the other students understood why Amy had divided 64 by each possible factor, so she asked, "You divided 64 by 1 and got 64. Can you show us what that rectangle looks like?" Amy then pointed to her picture of a rectangle that was 1×64. This process was repeated for each factor of 64. When Ms. Friedman asked Amy why she had "added up all the sides," Amy replied, "to figure out how much fencing was needed."

Nearly every group had found all four of the rectangles with whole number dimensions, and they all agreed that the 8 × 8 dimensions would require the least amount of fencing. However, their justifications for this varied. Jeremy explained that fencing was measured by perimeter and the 8 × 8 rectangle had the smallest perimeter. Many of the students did not use the word perimeter, but they found the sum of the four sides of the yard to determine how much fencing was needed. Amanda explained that she could tell "just by looking" that the 8 × 8 rectangle required the least amount of fencing. Ms. Friedman asked her to clarify, and she explained that she could look, for example, at a 16 × 4 rectangle and see that each 16 ft. side was equivalent to two 8 ft. sides, so the two 16 ft. sides were equivalent to four 8 ft. sides and the remaining two 4 ft. sides were extra.

Ms. Friedman wanted to be sure that everyone understood when it was appropriate to find area and when finding the perimeter was necessary. She asked the class, "Why did Amy add up all the sides of her rectangles?" Several students replied that she was finding perimeter. Ms. Friedman then asked, "Why did she want to find the perimeter?" Stephen replied, "Because that's how you figure out how much fencing you need." Ms. Friedman then said, "Yes, and when you were multiplying 1 × 64, 2 × 32, etc. to find the dimensions of the playpen, what were you finding?" Several students responded together that they were finding area to see how to use the 64 square feet of sod. Ms. Friedman then pointed out that there was quite a difference between the 32 feet of fencing needed for the 8 × 8 yard and the 130 feet of fencing that would be needed for the 1 × 64 rectangle. She wanted to help students recognize the real-world relevance of this problem and how the amount of fencing might affect the time needed to build the fence or the cost of the fencing materials.

A few students had finished the problem quickly. Ms. Friedman asked them to explain and justify their solutions to her. Once she was certain that they understood the underlying concepts of the problem, she gave them the following second-tier problem:

> **If fencing costs $1.38 per foot, what is the least amount Mark will have to spend for a rectangular fence if he uses all of his sod? Don't forget to add the 6% sales tax.**

This challenge problem required students to use results from the original problem. They had to use the perimeter of the 8 ft. × 8 ft. yard to find the cost, including tax, of the fencing. Four students attempted the challenge problem, using calculators to correctly find the final price of the fence. By moving from group to group, Ms. Friedman was able to differentiate instruction by supporting struggling students and challenging those who would benefit from a more complex task.

About the Math

This task required students to recognize that 64 square feet of sod represented the area of the rectangle, so the product of the length and width of the rectangle must equal

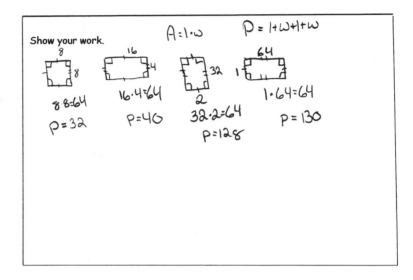

Mark's Puppy

Mark has 64 square feet of grass sod to make a fenced-in playpen for his new puppy. What are some possible rectangles that he could make with the sod? Which one will require the least amount of fencing?

Show your work.

$A = l \cdot w$ $P = l + w + l + w$

8 8·64   P=32

16·4=64   P=40

32·2=64   P=128

1·64=64   P=130

Explain how you solved the problem. Justify your answer.

8 by 8 would require the least amount of fencing because the rest of them have longer sides like 16 by 4. 8 by 8 only requires 32 feet of fencing. 16 by 4 = 40 feet of fencing. So 8 by 8 has lowest perimeter.

Figure 12–6 *Using words, pictures, and calculations, this student justifies his solution to the problem.*

64. Although most students found whole number factors of 64 to use as dimensions, a few considered non-whole number dimensions as well. Once they found possible rectangles with an area of 64 square feet, they then had to determine which rectangle required the least amount of fencing. This required them to recognize that determining the length of fencing needed for the playpen involved finding the perimeter, or the sum of the lengths of the four sides of the rectangle. In determining the measurements, students had to apply their computation skills as they multiplied, divided, and added to find the answers.

Problem-solving skills were also critical. Most students needed to picture the problem situation and began with a diagram of each possible playpen. After labeling the diagram with the measurements, students were better able to visualize and continue the task of determining how much fencing was needed. Students also recognized and applied formulas to the problem situation. The extension task, posed to the group who finished quickly, required students to find the final price for the fencing. These students applied both their understanding of operations and their calculator skills to determine the fencing cost. Through this problem exploration, students had opportunities to test and refine their understandings of area and perimeter measurement, as well as to practice their computation and calculator skills and to hone their problem-solving skills.

Problem Solving About Geometry

Students in grades 6 through 8 are building on their previous experiences with visualizing and drawing lines, angles, and polygons. They are now ready to investigate more sophisticated relationships such as overlapping angles and triangles. This can lead to further explorations involving similarity, congruency, and other geometry concepts. The following task explores the concept of overlapping angles. Students are challenged to use their problem-solving skills to organize and name all angles sharing a common vertex.

The Problem Task

Name all the angles shown here. Be sure that you name each angle only once.

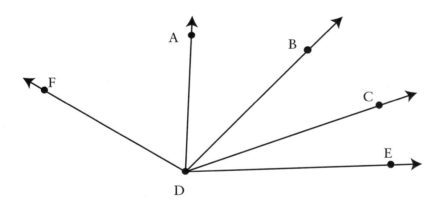

Mrs. Harlin began the lesson by sharing the problem with the class and then asking, "How do we name an angle?" One student responded that we have names for angles, like acute and obtuse. Mrs. Harlin used this as an opportunity to review the meanings of acute, right, and obtuse angles, asking her students to clarify each term. Then she told the class, "I'm thinking of a way to name an angle so that you know exactly which angle I mean." Most of the students remembered that naming an angle involved points, so Mrs. Harlin asked, "How many points does it take to name an angle?" Several students responded that it took three points. When Mrs. Harlin asked for an example, Antonio asked, "Angle *DFA*?" Mrs. Harlin asked Antonio to show her which angle he meant. Antonio pointed to ∠*FDA*, with a vertex at point *D*. Mrs. Harlin responded, "Points *D, F,* and *A* are three points that we can use to name that angle, but what needs to be changed?" Several students said that it should be named ∠*FDA*, not ∠*DFA*. Mrs. Harlin asked if there was another way to name that angle that would also be correct. Alicia replied that it could also be called ∠*ADF*. Mrs. Harlin asked the class why this angle could be called ∠*ADF* or ∠*FDA*, but not ∠*DFA*. Alicia responded that point *D* had to be in the middle. This led to a discussion about how an angle is the union of two rays, and that point *D* was where the rays met. When Mrs. Harlin asked what we call this point, several students responded in unison "The vertex!"

Students were warned that they would have to be careful not to name the same angle more than once. Mrs. Harlin then posed this question: Do you think that there are more than four different angles shown? Several students responded that more than four different angles were shown, while others seemed to question this. Mrs. Harlin suggested that students work in small groups to discuss their ideas and solve the problem.

As she circulated from group to group, Mrs. Harlin overheard discussions about whether or not there were more than four angles. The few students who believed that there were only four angles were quickly convinced that this was not the case. As soon as a fifth angle was identified, everyone was convinced.

After a few minutes, one student raised his hand and said that he had found six angles. Before Mrs. Harlin could respond, another student informed him that there were more than six. Mrs. Harlin urged them to "keep looking." Another student brought his paper to Mrs. Harlin. On it, he had listed the following angles: *FDA, FDB, FDC, FDE*. Mrs. Harlin asked him how he had come up with these angles. He replied that he had started with points *F* and *D* and then listed all possible angles that began with *FD*. Mrs. Harlin suggested that he try the same strategy using a different beginning point. He still looked confused, so she said, "How about starting with points *A* and *D*? You could have ∠*ADB*, ∠*ADC*. What would come next?" He quickly responded, "Oh, I see! ∠*ADE!*"

Another group showed Mrs. Harlin that they had found lots of angles. She counted them and realized that they had more than 10, so she suggested that they go back and see if they had named some angles more than once. They assured her that this was not the case. She pointed to their listing of ∠*ADB* and asked them to show her this angle on the diagram. Then she pointed to ∠*BDA* on their list and asked them to show her that angle. They quickly realized that they had named several angles twice even though the names were not identical.

Mrs. Harlin noticed that different groups were using varied methods of identifying the angles. Although a few groups were just naming angles as they found them, most groups were using some sort of organized plan. As students shared their solution strategies with the class, they commented on how much easier the problem was for those who used a system as opposed to just looking for angles in a random fashion. They also realized that there were many different ways to organize and keep track of the different angles. Some groups used tables; others used organized lists or diagrams (see Figures 12–7 and 12–8).

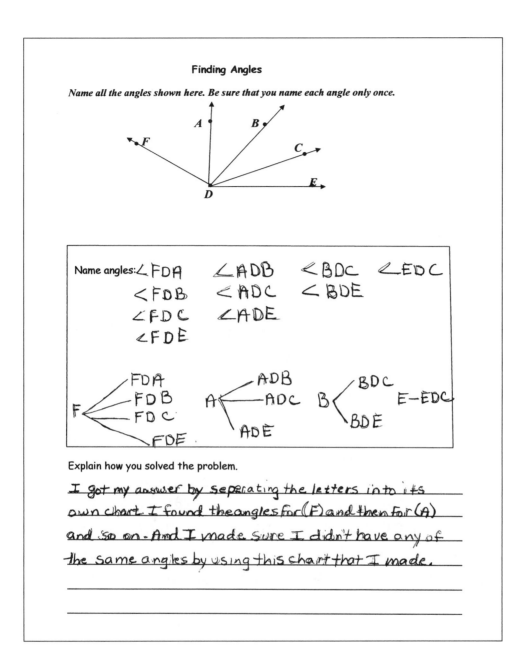

Figure 12–7 *This student used a tree diagram to organize her list of angles.*

About the Math

This task asked students to identify and name unique angles, including many that were overlapping. Students needed to use visualization, spatial sense, and geometric thinking. Many worked to create a system that would ensure that they named every angle and did not rename the same angle by reversing the order of the points. Sharing ideas with teams, and as a whole class, allowed them to identify and appreciate the different organizational systems that were used.

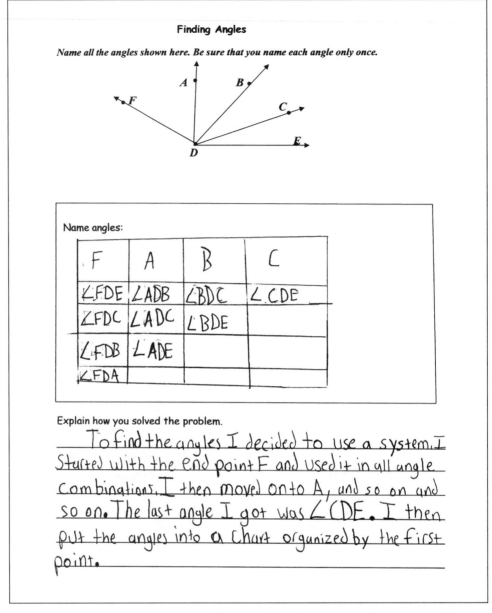

Finding Angles

Name all the angles shown here. Be sure that you name each angle only once.

Name angles:

F	A	B	C
∠FDE	∠ADB	∠BDC	∠CDE
∠FDC	∠ADC	∠BDE	
∠FDB	∠ADE		
∠FDA			

Explain how you solved the problem.

To find the angles I decided to use a system. I Started with the end point F and used it in all angle combinations. I then moved onto A, and so on and so on. The last angle I got was ∠CDE. I then put the angles into a chart organized by the first point.

Figure 12–8 *This student organized his list of overlapping angles using a table.*

Students used the diagram that was given. Some began by naming the four non-overlapping angles. Then many began to list angles that they saw when they combined two or three adjacent angles to make one larger angle. However, many quickly realized that this was an inefficient way of being sure that they named all angles. Several groups, once they realized that there was a pattern involved, found ways to organize their angles into lists, tables, or tree diagrams. Organizing the angles in this way helped them identify any angles that they had missed or had named twice. Their organizational skills and ability to visualize the task through tables, lists, and diagrams supported their ability to find the solutions. And persistence was an essential ingredient for success in this activity. While students found it easy to name the first four angles, the task got increasingly difficult, and sometimes frustrating, as they tried to find all of the angles.

Problem Solving About Data and Probability

Middle grades students are building on their understanding of basic probability concepts. Students in grades 6 through 8 are determining simple probabilities and learning to compute probabilities for compound events by using organized lists and tree diagrams. The following activity required students to consider such a problem.

The Problem Task

> **Chelsea the dog is expecting puppies. If Chelsea has four puppies, what is the probability that two of her puppies will be males and two will be females?**

An eighth-grade teacher, Miss Swanson, began by reviewing some basics of probability. She asked the students, "If you flip a coin, what are the possible outcomes?"

Everyone agreed that there were two possible outcomes: Heads or Tails. Then she asked, "What is the probability that the coin will land on Heads?" Nearly everyone responded with either "$\frac{1}{2}$" or "one out of two". Then Miss Swanson asked, "If you flip two coins, what are the possible outcomes?" There was some hesitation in responding, so Miss Swanson suggested that students discuss it with their partners.

MISS SWANSON: What is one possible outcome of flipping two coins?
STUDENT: We could get two Heads.
STUDENT: We could get two Tails.
STUDENT: We could get one of each.
MISS SWANSON: So how many different possibilities?
STUDENTS: Three.
MISS SWANSON: What if one of the coins is a nickel and the other a quarter? If the nickel landed on Heads and the quarter on Tails, would that be the same as the nickel landing on Tails and the quarter landing on Heads?
STUDENT: They would both be one Head and one Tail.
MISS SWANSON: Yes, but are they the same event? Did the outcome happen the same way?

The students agreed that they were actually two different outcomes, so there were really four possible outcomes. When Miss Swanson asked, "What is the probability that you will roll two Tails?" students quickly realized that it was $\frac{1}{4}$.

To help students connect the discussion about the coins with the current problem, Miss Swanson asked students to work with their partners to consider the following questions:

1. If puppy #1 is a male and puppies #2, 3, and 4 are female, is that the same event as puppies #1, 2, 3 being female and puppy #4 male?

2. What are all the different possible combinations of puppies that could be born?

Students immediately responded that the two events in the first question would be two separate events or outcomes. They then began tackling the second question. As they worked in pairs or small groups to determine the possible outcomes, Miss Swanson circulated around the room, listening, assessing, and offering assistance as needed. As she did, she noticed that many students were working to organize their ideas about possible outcomes using charts, diagrams, or lists. She remarked to the class, "I like the way a lot of you are considering ways to organize your ideas."

Michael showed Miss Swanson his paper, which had MMFF on it. Miss Swanson said, "Yes, that's one way it could happen, but there are more ways. What is another way?" Michael asked, "MFFF?" Miss Swanson replied, "Yes, but there are still more. Think of as many as you can." Then she said to the class, "I see that some of you are thinking of a combination and then checking to see if you already had that one, and others are using some sort of system to find the possibilities. One thing you will want to consider is how you will know when you have all of the possibilities listed. Remember that you want to make sure you have them all and that you haven't repeated any."

Miss Swanson looked at Leah's paper and saw that she had six possible outcomes listed. Miss Swanson asked Leah if she was using a system or just coming up with possibilities, and Leah indicated that she was thinking of possible outcomes in a random manner. Miss Swanson told a surprised Leah that she was missing over half of the possible outcomes. Then Miss Swanson told the class, "The number of possible outcomes is going to be more than you may think. Try to come up with some sort of system so you will know that you have all of them and no repeats. Is there a way to do that?" One student said, "Logic." Miss Swanson then asked, "Is there a way of logically ordering them?"

After several minutes, Miss Swanson determined that many students were having difficulty listing the possible combinations, so she decided to try an easier but related problem with them. She said, "If you are having trouble coming up with a plan, you might want to consider the possible outcomes for two puppies, then three puppies, and then four puppies." Through a whole-class discussion, students equated the case of two puppies with flipping two coins, which had already been discussed. They realized that the two puppies could be MM, MF, FM, or FF. Miss Swanson asked students to discuss with their partners how they could use these results to determine possible combinations of three, and then four, puppies.

Adam handed Miss Swanson his paper with 16 combinations listed. She asked, "Did you use any sort of logical plan or system to get them all or did you just try to come up with different combinations?" Adam said that he had not used a system. Miss Swanson replied, "So you might have repeated one. Go back and make sure you didn't repeat any." A short time later, Adam announced that he had indeed repeated one. Miss Swanson again suggested using an organized plan to ensure that students would find all combinations and not repeat any.

Miss Swanson noticed that Maria had used an interesting system to list her combinations, so she asked her to explain it to the class. Maria explained that she numbered the puppies, so her first combination was #1, 2, 3, 4 all males and then #1, 2, 3, 4 all females (Figure 12–9). Next, she listed #1 male and #2, 3, 4 females, and then she reversed this so that #1 was female and #2, 3, 4 were males. She continued to list

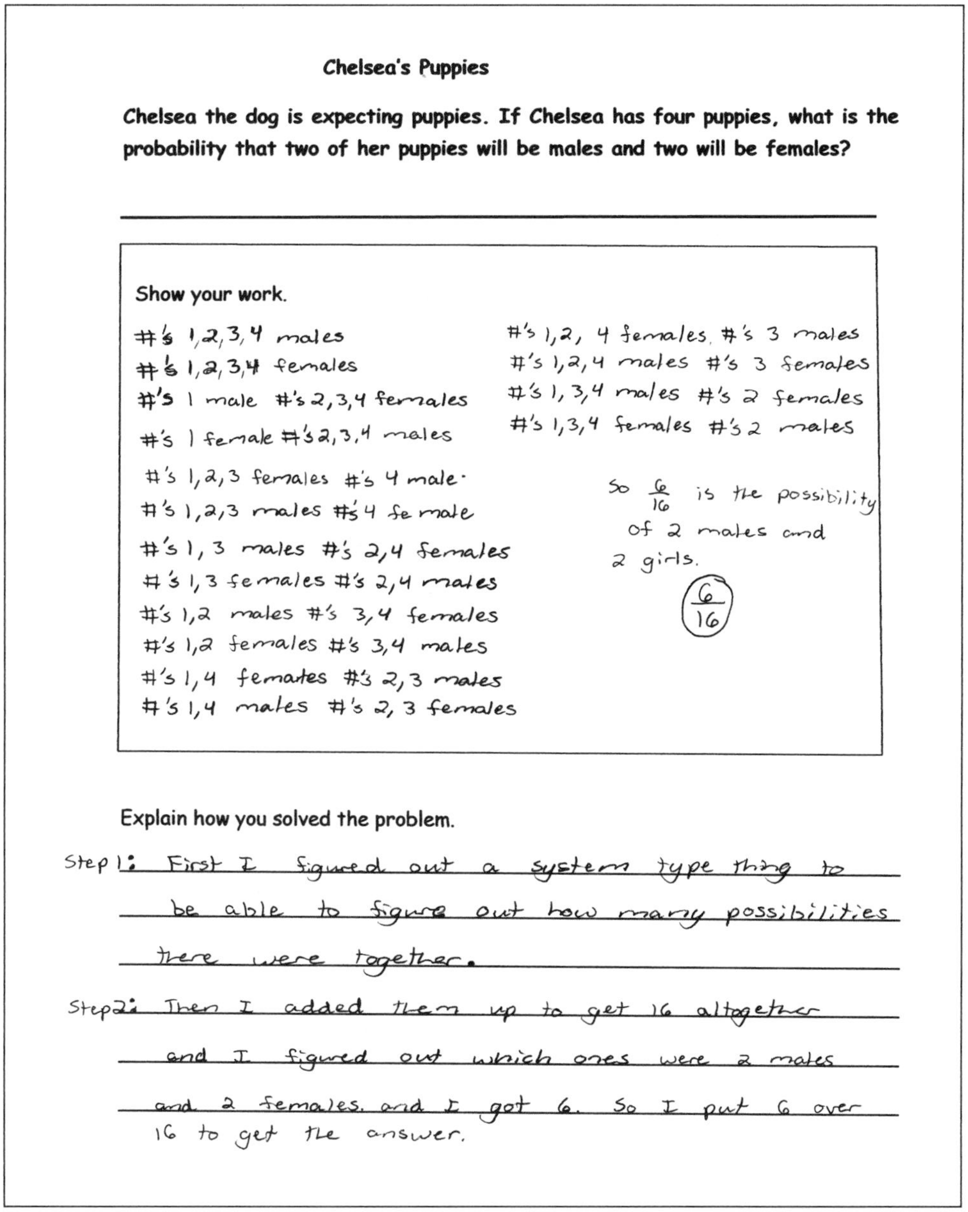

Chelsea's Puppies

Chelsea the dog is expecting puppies. If Chelsea has four puppies, what is the probability that two of her puppies will be males and two will be females?

Show your work.

#'s 1,2,3,4 males
#'s 1,2,3,4 females
#'s 1 male #'s 2,3,4 females
#'s 1 female #'s 2,3,4 males
#'s 1,2,3 females #'s 4 male.
#'s 1,2,3 males #'s 4 female
#'s 1,3 males #'s 2,4 females
#'s 1,3 females #'s 2,4 males
#'s 1,2 males #'s 3,4 females
#'s 1,2 females #'s 3,4 males
#'s 1,4 females #'s 2,3 males
#'s 1,4 males #'s 2,3 females

#'s 1,2, 4 females #'s 3 males
#'s 1,2,4 males #'s 3 females
#'s 1,3,4 males #'s 2 females
#'s 1,3,4 females #'s 2 males

So $\frac{6}{16}$ is the possibility
of 2 males and
2 girls.
$\boxed{\frac{6}{16}}$

Explain how you solved the problem.

Step 1: First I figured out a system type thing to be able to figure out how many possibilities there were together.

Step 2: Then I added them up to get 16 altogether and I figured out which ones were 2 males and 2 females. and I got 6. So I put 6 over 16 to get the answer.

Figure 12–9 *This student devised a system for listing all possible combinations by using numbers to represent puppies.*

all possibilities of one male and the other three female, and then she reversed each of these to indicate one female and three males. Then she listed all possible combinations of two males and two females in the same manner. For example, she listed #1, 2 male and #3, 4 female, and then she reversed these to have #1, 2 female and #3, 4 male. By doing this, she was able to see that there were 16 different possible outcomes.

Emily had also used a system to list her puppy combinations. She used a tree diagram that began with the first puppy: either M or F. From there, she added another branch for each additional puppy, again either M or F (Figure 12–10).

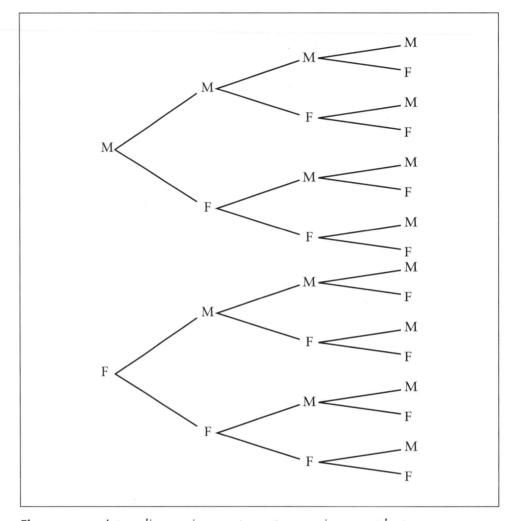

Figure 12–10 *A tree diagram is a great way to organize a sample space.*

Miss Swanson realized that many students had found all 16 combinations, so she reminded them that once they had found all the possibilities, they still had to find the probability of having 2 males and 2 females. Students went through their lists and made some sort of notation beside any combination comprising two males and two females. Some wrote the probability as $\frac{6}{16}$, while others simplified it to $\frac{3}{8}$, and two converted it to a decimal.

After students had finished, Miss Swanson asked for volunteers to share their solution with the class. As José wrote his list of possible combinations and explained how he had devised his plan, other students were checking off each combination on their own lists. Several voices could be heard saying, "Yep, I've got that one." As students explained their strategies, there were several different methods shared for listing possibilities in a logical, organized manner. Carlos wrote his list on the board. Miss Swanson commented, "I see that you used a system too." Carlos replied, "I didn't figure out that I had a system at first. I just did it." Miss Swanson assured him that this happens sometimes. "It's just your mind working logically," she told him. The class then worked together to discover what pattern Carlos had used.

After strategies had been shared, Miss Swanson asked, "There were 16 possibilities for four puppies. How many possibilities would there be with 5 puppies?"

STUDENT: There are 25 possibilities.

MISS SWANSON: How do you know?

STUDENT: With 4 puppies there were 16, which is 4 × 4, so with 5 puppies, there would be 5 × 5 or 25 possibilities.

MISS SWANSON: I like how you are looking for a pattern. That is one of our strategies. Let's look at the pattern in a chart.

As Miss Swanson drew the following (Figure 12–11) on the board, she asked students to help her fill in each of the cells in the table. Everyone agreed that there were only two possibilities for 1 puppy: male or female. Miss Swanson reminded students that they had already figured out the number of possibilities for two puppies earlier in the class, and they had just figured out that there were 16 possibilities for 4 puppies.

Miss Swanson then asked students to use this information to complete the missing cells. Students discussed how 2 × 2 = 4 and 4 × 4 = 16. Many were convinced that with 5 puppies, there would be 25 possibilities. Miss Swanson suggested that together the class figure out the number of possibilities with 3 puppies. Some students were sure that there would be 9 (3 × 3) possibilities, but Matthew said, "No, there would be 8 because it doubles each time. Two doubled is 4, and 4 doubled is 8, and 8 doubled is 16. There would be 16 doubled, or 32 possibilities for 5 puppies." Miss Swanson then asked the class, "Which pattern makes sense with puppies? Does it make sense that you would square the number of puppies to get the number of possibilities or does it make sense that you would double the number of possibilities with each additional puppy?" Brian responded, "It makes sense to double it. There are two possible outcomes each time. For each old outcome, there are two new outcomes." Miss Swanson recorded ideas on the board as she clarified, "Yes, if we have MMMM with 4 puppies, the 5th puppy would be either male or female, which would give us the two new possibilities: MMMMM or MMMMF." Miss Swanson had used the remaining few minutes of class to challenge students to use their results to determine and make sense of a pattern.

Number of Puppies	Number of Possibilities
1	2
2	4
3	?
4	16
5	?

Figure 12–11 *This teacher used a table to help students look for patterns.*

Figure 12–12 *Students share alternate solution methods with the class.*

About the Math

In order to determine the probability in this task, students had to understand the concept of probability and know that they needed to find the number of outcomes that fit a criterion (e.g., two male puppies and two female puppies) and the total number of outcomes (e.g., all of the possible outcomes for a litter of four puppies). Although students had no problem determining the simple probability of a coin toss, dealing with probabilities for compound events such as a litter of four puppies was much more complex.

In solving this problem, many students applied their understanding of organized lists. As they worked to determine the possible combinations of male and female puppies, many students began by listing MMMM, MMMF, MMFF, MFFF, and then repeating the same pattern in reverse beginning with FFFF. Others thought of one combination at a time, in a random fashion, but then reversed it. For example, a student who thought of the combination MFMF would then immediately also list FMFM. Another student used a tree diagram to keep track of possible combinations. After many trials where some combinations were either missing or repeated, nearly every student used some sort of strategy in listing possible combinations. To complete this activity, students were required to blend their understanding of simple probability with probability of compound events. In doing so, they applied the problem-solving strategies of using logical reasoning, finding patterns, and making organized lists. Throughout the task, they were supported by teacher questioning and benefited from the ability to talk and work with their peers.

Linking Problem Solving and Math Content

Problem-solving activities provide students with opportunities to explore math content and expand their understanding of that content, to apply math skills to problem situations, and to practice their use of problem-solving strategies. Whether problems focus on numbers and operations, algebra, geometry, measurement, or data and probability, students benefit from opportunities to explore math content through problems. When problem-solving tasks are carefully selected, they serve to expand and refine students' understanding of the problem-solving process as well as their understanding of math content.

Questions for Discussion

1. How are problem-solving skills reinforced during these tasks?

2. What should the teacher consider when selecting problem tasks? What considerations during planning would result in more effective problem-solving lessons?

3. How does integrating content and process enhance student learning?

4. In what ways should teachers support students as they engage in problem-solving lessons?

5. How might the teacher support struggling students and challenge gifted students during problem tasks?

Accepting the Challenge

Teaching mathematics well is a complex endeavor; and there are no easy recipes.

—National Council of Teachers of Mathematics,
Principles and Standards for School Mathematics

Teaching students to become effective problem solvers is both the goal and the challenge of mathematics instruction in the middle grades. The goal is for students to solve problems, not to perform isolated math drills. The problem-solving process helps students to recognize the meaningfulness of the math we teach, identify ways to apply math skills to find solutions to problems, and gain greater insight into the mathematics they are exploring. Problem solving engages students in the study of mathematics. It motivates them, stimulates their curiosity, and helps them gain insights.

But problem solving is challenging for our students, as it requires them to understand math skills and concepts while developing the thinking skills necessary to apply those skills and concepts to problem situations. Problem solving is not something that can be memorized. Each problem task requires thought, discussion, planning, and an understanding of which math skills to apply and how to apply them to solve the problem.

We are beginning to recognize the importance of teaching through problem solving, of allowing students to explore math ideas through problem tasks. And we are recognizing the importance of focusing on the teaching of problem-solving skills to support students as they develop a repertoire of strategies for approaching problems. We have identified skills and strategies that guide students through the problem-solving process and assist them in organizing needed data. Discussions, group work, and writing in mathematics class have allowed students to share their thinking processes and strengthen their understanding of the skills they are acquiring.

Working Together to Build Effective Problem Solvers

Students benefit from ongoing experiences with problem solving, and schools that work together to support students' problem-solving skills are able to offer students the consistency of a problem-solving focus across grade levels. When students explore math through problem tasks and discuss their problem-solving skills from year to year, they are able to build on prior experiences and refine their understandings. It is our individual responsibility, as well as a school responsibility, to develop our students' problem-solving skills, refine our teaching skills, and provide the most appropriate math education for our students.

Working to Refine Our Skills

Many of us had minimal experience with math problem solving when we were students in the math classroom. Many adults report that they rarely discussed problems, were not taught strategies, learned math skills in isolation, and focused on computations rather than problem solving. While we recognize the importance of problem solving and the need to support our students with problem-solving experiences, it can be challenging to change instructional approaches that are deeply rooted in our own past experiences. And to attempt the change on our own can be daunting. In many schools, teachers are recognizing the benefits of working together to develop a model of an effective teacher of math problem solving. Through co-planning, lesson sharing, professional development sessions, and teacher study groups, we are supporting each other as we develop our skills at teaching math problem solving.

CLASSROOM-TESTED TIP

Refining Our Instructional Practices

Our goal as teachers is to continue to strengthen our instructional skills to meet the changing needs of our students. To become an effective teacher of math problem solving, we are challenged to find ways to expand and refine our skills as we help students develop this critical math process. Try these activities to continue to refine your teaching skills:

■ Read a piece of professional literature and reflect on it as you think about your own experiences in the classroom.

- Look carefully at your students' work. Look for evidence of what they know and clues for how you can help them improve their skills.

- Try new techniques and activities and then reflect on the outcomes. If they are not immediately successful, modify the activities or your delivery of the activities to find the best approach for your students.

- Find a colleague with whom you can discuss ideas, share experiences, or even observe each other's teaching.

- When planning math lessons, consider ways to incorporate problem-solving activities related to all content standards.

Many teachers applaud the benefits of working in teams. Grade level, or other planning teams, provide teachers with an opportunity to discuss and co-plan instructional activities with colleagues. Team meetings offer a chance to share resources (e.g., materials, lesson plans), or provide a forum to generate lesson ideas. Teachers can work together to develop a problem task to set a context for an upcoming math concept, analyze samples of student work with colleagues, or debrief after problem experiences to share successes and brainstorm ways to avoid difficulties or clarify misunderstandings. Teaming, whether formal or informal, allows us to share ideas, refine our understandings, and grow as teachers.

The Role of the Administrator

The school or district administrator plays a key role in the development of teachers' skills. Providing ongoing professional development is a critical responsibility of administrators. Professional development comes in many shapes and sizes. Teachers benefit from workshops on problem-solving approaches in which new ideas are shared or teaching techniques are modeled. Workshops can infuse new ideas into a staff and are most valuable when there are several sessions, each building upon the others and allowing for teacher reflection. Many schools support the viewing of videotaped classroom lessons (either commercial products or informal tapes made within the school) to provide teachers with examples of teaching methods and to stimulate discussion about the techniques and activities presented in the videotaped lessons. Videos allow teachers to view teaching techniques in action.

Faculty study groups have become a very popular form of professional development because of their ongoing format as well as their potential for encouraging reflection about practice. Study groups might take the form of book studies in which teachers select a relevant piece of professional literature to read and discuss with colleagues over a series of meetings, or might simply be groups of teachers that meet to explore a component of instruction (e.g., math problem solving). A group facilitator guides the discussions and encourages teachers to try related activities in their classrooms, bring student work samples to sessions, or share reflections based on their own practice. Study groups place value on teachers' experiences and enhance those experiences through readings and subsequent discussions. Study groups sometimes evolve into inquiry groups in which teachers explore a key question about problem solving or action research groups in which they gather data and discuss their findings.

The school administrator has the ability to set priorities within the building. Through observations of teaching practice, the administrator can monitor and enhance teaching behaviors. Through the selection of topics for faculty meetings or professional development sessions, administrators can show the importance of math problem solving. Through the designation of a school-based math leader, specialist, or coach, administrators can be reassured that math goals will remain a priority and faculty will receive support and encouragement as they work to refine their skills. Through providing opportunities for discussions with colleagues, peer observations, and study groups, administrators can continue to enhance teacher effectiveness.

Meeting the Needs of All Students

Working together in a school-wide effort to enhance students' problem-solving skills requires attention to all students within the school. Discussions should focus on ways to support struggling students, as well as strategies for extending the problem-solving skills of gifted students. Resource teachers and specialists play a key role in school-wide growth. Specialists with expertise in gifted education, learning disabilities, or English language learners can provide valuable insights into ways to modify instruction to meet the specific needs of these students. Having all faculty assembled to discuss possible strategies will allow specialists to offer tips based on their specific knowledge.

Differentiating instruction to meet the needs of all students is critical in the teaching of problem solving. Understanding key thinking skills and problem-solving strategies, and the way these strategies develop from simple to more complex, is fundamental knowledge that allows us to differentiate our instruction. As we observe students' skills and determine their level of understanding, knowledge of the progression of problem-solving skills will allow us to present simpler problems for students who need to develop foundation skills or extend problems for those who are ready to be challenged.

The Challenge to Educators

The NCTM Problem-Solving Process Standard guides our efforts to redefine our classroom instruction. As the central focus of the mathematics curriculum (NCTM 1989), problem solving deserves focus and attention within our classrooms, and problem-solving experiences must become a part of our daily mathematics practices. Through the development of a positive classroom climate, we allow our students to test their skills and extend their thinking in a safe, comfortable environment that supports risk taking and creative thinking. Through hands-on and visual teaching techniques, we enable our students to explore problem solving and begin to build a repertoire of strategies and skills to allow them to tackle even complex problems. Through think-aloud techniques, we share our thinking to allow students to see into our heads as they try to understand how to think like problem solvers. Through group and partner work, we allow students to verbalize their ideas, hear the ideas of others, and build on their understanding as they consider new ideas. Through a variety of practice activities, our students are able to extend and refine their skills. And through opportunities for students to identify and assess their own thinking strategies (metacognition), we show students the power of understanding their own thinking.

The National Council of Teachers of Mathematics, through their *Principles and Standards* (2000), has provided us with a guide to help our students develop as math problem solvers. When we understand the problem-solving process standard and see how it relates to the content standards, we can effectively integrate our teaching of math problem solving with our teaching of other math skills and concepts. We can support students to understand and apply their content skills and help them develop problem-solving strategies to solve a variety of math problems.

Our goal as math educators is to acquire skills and strategies to help our students grow as mathematical thinkers. We are challenged to experiment with new strategies and techniques within our classroom to allow students to visualize and experience problem-solving situations. We are challenged to encourage students to communicate their ideas, discuss alternate solutions, and monitor their own thinking processes. We are challenged to present new math ideas in problem contexts to allow students to build on their prior understandings through the active exploration of math concepts. We are challenged to stimulate students with thought-provoking, open-ended problems and guide our students toward reasonable solutions. We are challenged to create a classroom in which our students investigate, explore, reason, and communicate about problem solving on a daily basis and in which they can grow to become confident and capable problem solvers.

CLASSROOM-TESTED TIP

School-wide Focus

Consider working together within your school to strengthen the problem-solving skills of students at all grade levels. Make problem solving a priority within your math classrooms. Try these school-wide activities:

- Develop school-wide programs to motivate students (e.g., Problem-of-the-Week announcements or school-wide math challenges).

- Create a school-wide problem-solving bulletin board to highlight exemplary samples of student work across all grade levels.

- Send problem-solving tips home in a parent newsletter or post them on a school website.

- Inventory supplies and manipulatives in your building and find a system for sharing them among colleagues.

- Hold a problem-solving family math night or discuss the importance of problem solving at your school's Back-to-School Night.

- Begin a problem-solving book study group or focus group for teachers in your school.

Questions for Discussion

1. What are the benefits of a school-wide focus on math problem solving? How might you help to create a school-wide focus?

2. In what ways can you improve your skills at teaching problem solving?

3. How does teaming support classroom teachers? In what ways can classroom teachers and specialists work together to support students as they learn to solve problems?

4. What is the role of the school administrator in developing teachers' understanding of the NCTM problem-solving standard? How might all teachers be supported to better understand the teaching of math problem solving?

Additional Resources for Problem Solving

The following resources are meant to support you as you continue to explore the problem-solving standard in grades 6 through 8. You will find a variety of text resources—books that will provide you with additional problem-solving activities or instructional strategies. A list of math websites is included to supply you with problem tasks, electronic manipulative ideas, or teacher resources. And for additional professional development, several video products are listed that allow you to view problem solving in classrooms and reflect on the video lessons alone or with a group of your colleagues.

Text Resources

The following text resources provide a variety of activities and strategies for supporting students as they develop their problem-solving skills:

Burns, M. 1992. *About Teaching Mathematics*. Sausalito, CA: Math Solutions.

Burns, M., and C. Humphreys. 1990. *A Collection of Math Lessons, Grades 6–8*. Sausalito, CA: Math Solutions.

Charles, R. I., and E. A. Silver, eds. 1989. *The Teaching and Assessing of Mathematical Problem Solving*. Reston, VA: National Council of Teachers of Mathematics.

Coburn, T. G. 1993. *NCTM Addenda Series—Patterns*. Reston, VA: National Council of Teachers of Mathematics.

Lester, F. K., and R. I. Charles, eds. 2003. *Teaching Mathematics Through Problem Solving: Prekindergarten–Grade 6*. Reston, VA: National Council of Teachers of Mathematics.

National Council of Teachers of Mathematics. 1989. *Curriculum and Evaluation Standards for School Mathematics*. Reston, VA: National Council of Teachers of Mathematics.

———. 1991. *Professional Standards for Teaching Mathematics*. Reston, VA: National Council of Teachers of Mathematics.

———. 1995. *Assessment Standards for School Mathematics*. Reston, VA: National Council of Teachers of Mathematics.

————. 2000. *Principles and Standards for School Mathematics.* Reston, VA: National Council of Teachers of Mathematics.

O'Connell, S. 2001. *Math—The Write Way for Grades 6–7.* Columbus, OH: Frank Schaffer Publications.

————. 2005. *Now I Get It: Strategies for Building Confident and Competent Mathematicians K–6.* Portsmouth, NH: Heinemann.

Post, B., and S. Eads. 1996. *Logic, Anyone?* Torrance, CA: Fearon Teacher Aids.

Schoenfield, M., and J. Rosenblatt. 1985. *Discovering Logic (Grades 4–6).* Grand Rapids, MI: Fearon Teacher Aids.

Stenmark, J. Kerr, ed. 1995. *101 Short Problems from EQUALS.* Berkeley, CA: Regents of the University of California.

Van de Walle, J., and L. H. Lovin. 2005. *Teaching Student-Centered Mathematics, Grades 5–8.* New York: Pearson Education, Inc.

Whitin, D. J., and R. Cox. 2003. *A Mathematical Passage: Strategies for Promoting Inquiry in Grades 4–6.* Portsmouth, NH: Heinemann.

Web Resources

The following websites provide a variety of lesson ideas, classroom resources, and ready-to-use problem-solving tasks:

www.abcteach.com/directory/basics/math/problem_solving/
The abcteach website has problem-solving activities from PreK through 8th grade. Some are free; others require site membership.

www.aimsedu.org/index.html
AIMS (Activities Integrating Mathematics and Science) offers sample activities, information on AIMS professional development, an online store, and other teacher resources.

www.eduplace.com/math/brain/index.html
The Houghton Mifflin website contains brain teasers for grades 3 through 8 as well as an archive of past problems.

www.etacuisenaire.com
ETA/Cuisenaire is a supplier of classroom mathematics manipulatives and teacher resource materials.

www.heinemann.com
The website of Heinemann Publishing Company provides a variety of professional development resources for teachers.

www.illuminations.nctm.org
Explore a variety of problem-based lessons on this website of the National Council of Teachers of Mathematics.

www.learner.org/resources/series190.html
This Annenberg Media site offers a free, self-paced online course to help teachers better understand the NCTM Process Standards and find effective ways to integrate the process standards with their content teaching.

www.learningresources.com
This website of the Learning Resources Company offers a variety of mathematics manipulatives and teacher resource materials.

www.math.com/teachers.html

This site offers lesson plans, classroom resources, links to "free stuff," problems of the week, worksheet generators, and online tutorial assistance.

www.mathforum.org

This website has a problem of the week component that offers feedback from mentors on problem-solving and communication skills. There is a fee to subscribe.

http://mathforum.org/discussions/

This website offers a list of discussion forums by subject area. Teachers post problems or discussion topics so that others can reply with solutions or responses.

www.nctm.org

On this National Council of Teachers of Mathematics (NCTM) website you will find information on regional and national conferences sponsored by NCTM, as well as a variety of professional development materials.

www.tomsnyder.com

This Tom Snyder Productions website sells commercial problem-solving software products listed by grade level.

www.whitehouse.gov/kids/math/

This site offers White House Kids math challenges at elementary and middle school levels.

Staff Development Training Videos

The following professional development training videos feature a problem-solving focus for teaching mathematics and offer tips and strategies for teaching math problem solving. These video programs allow teachers to view problem solving in action in middle grades classrooms. Videos are accompanied by manuals with reflection questions and activity ideas.

Burns, M. 1989. *Mathematics: for Middle School.* Vernon Hills, IL: ETA Cuisenaire (www.etacuisenaire.com).

Increasing Students' Math Problem-Solving Skills Part I: Developing Core Problem-Solving Strategies, Grades 3–6. 2004. Bellevue, WA: Bureau of Education and Research (www.ber.org).

Increasing Students' Math Problem-Solving Skills Part II: Expanding Students' Repertoire of Problem-Solving Strategies, Grades 3–6. 2004. Bellevue, WA: Bureau of Education and Research (www.ber.org).

Burns, M. 1982. *Math for Smarty Pants*. Boston: Little, Brown & Co.

———. 1992. *About Teaching Mathematics*. New York: Math Solutions.

Charles, R. I., and E. A. Silver, eds. 1989. *The Teaching and Assessing of Mathematical Problem Solving*. Reston, VA: National Council of Teachers of Mathematics.

Coburn, T. G. 1993. *NCTM Addenda Series—Patterns*. Reston, VA: National Council of Teachers of Mathematics.

Forsten, C. 1992. *Teaching Thinking and Problem Solving in Math*. New York: Scholastic.

Hiebert, J. 1999. "Relationships Between Research and the NCTM Standards." *Journal for Research in Mathematics Education* 30 (1): 3–19.

Hiebert, J., T. Carpenter, E. Fennema, K. Fuson, D. Wearne, H. Murray, A. Olivier, and P. Human. 1997. *Making Sense: Teaching and Learning Mathematics with Understanding*. Portsmouth, NH: Heinemann.

Kilpatrick, J., W. G. Martin, and D. Schifter, eds. 2003. *A Research Companion to Principles and Standards for School Mathematics*. Reston, VA: National Council of Teachers of Mathematics.

Lester, F., and R. Charles, eds. 2003. *Teaching Mathematics Through Problem Solving: Prekindergarten–Grade 6*. Reston, VA: National Council of Teachers of Mathematics.

National Council of Teachers of Mathematics. 1989. *Curriculum and Evaluation Standards for School Mathematics*. Reston, VA: Author.

———. 1991. *Professional Standards for Teaching Mathematics*. Reston, VA: Author.

———. 1995. *Assessment Standards for School Mathematics*. Reston, VA: Author.

———. 2000. *Principles and Standards for School Mathematics*. Reston, VA: Author.

O'Connell, S. R. 1992. "Math Pairs—Parents as Partners." Arithmetic Teacher 40 (1): 10–12.

———. 2001. *Math—The Write Way for Grades 6-7*. Columbus, OH: Frank Schaffer Publications.

———. 2005. *Now I Get It: Strategies for Building Confident and Competent Mathematicians K–6*. Portsmouth, NH: Heinemann.

Polya, G. 2004. *How To Solve It: A New Aspect of Mathematical Method*, 3rd ed. Princeton, NJ: Princeton University Press.

Sowder, L. 2002. "Story Problems and Students' Strategies." In *Putting Research into Practice in the Elementary Grades*. Reston, VA: National Council of Teachers of Mathematics (pp. 21–23).

Stenmark, J. K., ed. 1991. *Mathematics Assessment—Myths, Models, Good Questions, and Practical Suggestions*. Reston, VA: National Council of Teachers of Mathematics.

Van de Walle, J. A. 2004. *Elementary and Middle School Mathematics: Teaching Developmentally*. New York: Pearson Education.

Van de Walle, J. A., and L. H. Lovin. 2005. *Teaching Student-Centered Mathematics, Grades 5-8*. Boston: Pearson Education.

Whitin, D., and R. Cox. 2003. *A Mathematical Passage: Strategies for Promoting Inquiry in Grades 4–6*. Portsmouth, NH: Heinemann.

Whitin, P., and D. Whitin. 2000. *Math Is Language Too: Talking and Writing in the Mathematics Classroom*. Urbana, IL: National Council of Teachers of English.

Why Are Student Activities on a CD?

At first glance, the CD included with this book appears to be a collection of teaching tools and student activities, much like the activities that appear in many teacher resource books. But rather than taking a book to the copier to copy an activity, the CD allows you to simply print off the desired page on your home or work computer. No more standing in line at the copier or struggling to carefully position the book on the copier so you can make a clean copy. And with our busy schedules, we appreciate having activities that are classroom ready and aligned with our math standards.

You may want to simplify some tasks or add complexity to others. The problems on the CD often include several parts or have added challenge extensions. When it is appropriate for your students, simply delete these sections, for a quick way to simplify or shorten the tasks. Here are some examples of ways you may want to change the tasks and why. A more complete version of this guide with more samples for editing the activities can be found on the CD-ROM.

Editing the CD to Motivate and Engage Students

Personalizing Tasks or Capitalizing on Students' Interests

The editable forms on the CD provide a quick and easy way to personalize math problems. Substituting students' names, the teacher's name, a favorite restaurant, sports team, or location can immediately engage students. You know the interests of your students. Mentioning their interests in your problems is a great way to increase their enthusiasm for the activities. Think about their favorite activities and simply substitute their interests for those that might appear in the problems. In the second version of the example that follows, the teacher knows that many of her students play soccer and decides to reword the task to capture their interest. *Note:* This type of editing is also important when the problem situation may not be culturally appropriate for your students (i.e., your school may not hold dances).

Name _____

Valentine's Day Dance

The eighth grade is planning a Valentine's Day Dance in the school gym. There will be 98 people attending the dance. The school has 3 rectangular tables that each seat 8. They also have round tables that seat 5 and square tables that seat 4. How can they select tables to use so that they use the least number of tables?

_____ rectangular tables, _____ round tables, _____ square tables = _____ total tables

Show your work.

Explain how you solved this problem.

_____
_____
_____
_____
_____
_____
_____

May be copied for classroom use. © 2008 by Joy Bronston Schackow and Susan O'Connell from *Introduction to Problem Solving: Grades 6–8* (Heinemann: Portsmouth, NH).

Name _____

Soccer Banquet

The soccer league is planning a banquet for the players and their families in the school gym. There will be 98 people attending the banquet. The school has 3 rectangular tables that each seat 8. They also have round tables that seat 5 and square tables that seat 4. How can they select tables to use so that they use the least number of tables?

_____ rectangular tables, _____ round tables, _____ square tables, _____ total tables =

Show your work.

Explain how you solved this problem.

_____
_____
_____
_____
_____
_____
_____

May be copied for classroom use. © 2008 by Joy Bronston Schackow and Susan O'Connell from *Introduction to Problem Solving: Grades 6–8* (Heinemann: Portsmouth, NH).

Editing the CD to Differentiate Instruction

Creating Shortened or Tiered Tasks

While many students are able to move from one task to another, some students benefit from focusing on one task at a time. By simply separating parts of a task, teachers can help focus students on the first part of the task before moving them to the second part. Teachers might choose to provide all students with the first task and then give students the second part after they have completed it and had their work checked by the teacher. In this sample, the two parts of the task, which initially appeared on one page together, have been separated and the space between the lines for writing responses has been widened for students who may need more writing space.

Name _____

Sharing Pizza

1. Terrance and his sister shared a pizza. They ate $\frac{5}{8}$ of the pizza altogether. If Terrance ate $\frac{1}{4}$ of the pizza, how much did his sister eat? _____

Show your work.

Explain how you solved the problem.

_____
_____
_____
_____

---

2. Terrance's brother decided to share some pizza with Terrance and his sister. If Terrance ate $\frac{1}{4}$ of the pizza, his brother ate $\frac{3}{16}$ of the pizza, and altogether the three ate $\frac{5}{8}$ of the pizza, how much pizza did Terrance's sister eat?

Show your work.

Explain how you solved the problem.

_____
_____
_____
_____
_____
_____

Adding some fun details can generate interest and excitement in story problems, but you might prefer to modify some problems for students with limited reading ability. Simply deleting some of the words on the editable CD will result in an easy-to-read version of the same task.

Name _____

Healthy Habits

Mrs. Birch's class was studying health and fitness. Every student decided on a plan to get healthier.

1. Danny decided to get more exercise. He rode his bike $2\frac{3}{4}$ miles each day for 9 days. How many miles did he ride? _____

Show your work.

2. Kathy decided to eat less candy. She ate 81 pieces of candy last month and she ate only $\frac{3}{4}$ as much this month. How many pieces of candy did she eat this month? _____

Show your work.

3. Lisa decided to drink 4 bottles of water a day. Each bottle holds 16.9 ounces. How many ounces of water did she drink in a week? _____

Show your work.

Explain how you figured out how much water Lisa drank in a week.

_____

_____

_____

_____

_____

_____

_____

May be copied for classroom use. © 2008 by Joy Bronston Schackow and Susan O'Connell from *Introduction to Problem Solving: Grades 6–8* (Heinemann: Portsmouth, NH).

Name _____

Healthy Habits

1. Danny rode his bike $2\frac{3}{4}$ miles each day for 9 days. How many miles did he ride? _____

Show your work.

2. Katy ate 81 pieces of candy last month and $\frac{2}{3}$ as much this month. How many pieces of candy did she eat this month? _____

Show your work.

3. Lisa drinks 4 bottles of water a day. Each bottle holds 16.9 ounces. How many ounces of water did she drink in a week? _____

Show your work.

Explain how you got your answer.

_____

_____

_____

_____

_____

_____

_____

_____

May be copied for classroom use. © 2008 by Joy Bronston Schackow and Susan O'Connell from *Introduction to Problem Solving: Grades 6–8* (Heinemann: Portsmouth, NH).

Modifying Data

Although all students may work on the same problem task, modifying the problem data will allow teachers to create varying versions of the task. Using the editable forms on the CD, you can either simplify the data or insert more challenging data including larger numbers, fractions, decimals, or percents.

Name _____

Scoring Baskets

1. Brian scored 16 points in the first basketball game of the season. He scored 13 points in the second and 9 points in the third. How many points did he score in the fourth game if his scoring average for the first four games of the season was 15?

_____

Show your work.

Explain how you solved the problem.

_____
_____
_____
_____
_____

2. How many total points did Brian score in his next game if his average for the first five games of the season was 14? Explain how you figured it out.

_____
_____

Name _____

Scoring Baskets

1. Brian scored 16 points in the first basketball game of the season. He scored 13 points in the second, 15 points in the third, 10 points in the fourth, and 8 points in the fifth game. How many points did he score in the sixth game if his scoring average for the first six games of the season was 13.5?

_____

Show your work.

Explain how you solved the problem.

_____
_____
_____
_____
_____

2. How many total points did Brian score in his next two games if his average for the first eight games of the season was 14.5? Explain how you figured it out.

_____
_____